MW01009989

COUNTRY HOUSES
OF ENGLAND

LANDHÄUSER
IN ENGLAND

LES MAISONS
ROMANTIQUES
D'ANGLETERRE

COUNTRY HOUSES OF ENGLAND

LANDHÄUSER IN ENGLAND

LES MAISONS ROMANTIQUES D'ANGLETERRE

Barbara & René Stoeltie

EDITED BY · HERAUSGEGEBEN VON · SOUS LA DIRECTION DE
Angelika Taschen

TASCHEN

KÖLN LONDON MADRID NEW YORK PARIS TOKYO

CONTENTS
INHALT
SOMMAIRE

ROMANTIC
COUNTRY HOUSES
OF ENGLAND

John Constable, *Ann Constable* (1800/5 or 1815), Tate Gallery, London

ABOVE · OBEN · CI-DESSUS: John Constable, *The White Horse · Das weiße Pferd · Le Cheval blanc* (1819), The Frick Collection, New York

Our ideal of the majestic beauty of the English countryside stems from an early encounter with the hilly landscapes immortalised by Gainsborough, Turner and Constable – those landscapes so buffeted by strong winds that the very trees seem hunched against the head-long, cloud-filled sky.

The charm – as opposed to the beauty – of rural England may have touched us for the first time otherwise and more delicately, one day when we found ourselves staring at a great Palladian house in the midst of a broad park dotted with statues and follies; or again, when we experienced the visual shock of a simple cottage with a thatched roof, whose reflected outline lay trembling on the mirror-surface of a river.

Indeed England and the English countryside are so closely associated in our minds as to be indivisible, for in the green landscapes of this island it is commonplace to turn a corner and see before you an 18th-century manor in the purest Georgian style, or a Gothic-looking rectory built two centuries back. Perhaps the rectory will stand at the edge of a village adjoining a crumbling church and a graveyard with moss-laden gravestones; and perhaps in this village there will be an oak-panelled pub which can offer the hungry traveller a glass of ale and a piping hot shepherd's pie…

ROMANTISCHE LANDHÄUSER IN ENGLAND

John Constable,
Golding Constable
(1815), Tate Gallery,
London

Wer die Schönheit der englischen Landschaft kennt, hat unweigerlich die sanften, leuchtend grünen Hügel vor Augen, die sich bei der ersten Begegnung mit ihnen ins Gedächtnis geradezu eingebrannt haben. Gainsborough, Turner und Constable haben diese Landschaft in ihren Gemälden verewigt und festgehalten, wie der Wind unerbittlich gegen knorrige Bäume und Äste schlägt, die sich vor dem wolkenschweren Himmel zu ducken scheinen.

Sich den idyllischeren Charme der englischen Landschaft vor Augen zu führen, bedeutet, sich an den Tag zu erinnern, als man vor einem palladianischen Landsitz stand, umgeben von einem riesigen Park mit zahlreichen Statuen und Ziergebäuden. Oder sich der seltsamen Rührung zu entsinnen, die man beim Anblick eines einfachen Cottage empfand, dessen Silhouette mit dem strohgedeckten Dach sich silbern in einem gewundenen Bach spiegelte.

Wer von England spricht, meint das Leben auf dem Land. In dieser sattgrünen Landschaft kommt es nicht selten vor, daß man plötzlich vor einem georgianischen Herrenhaus aus dem 18. Jahrhundert steht oder überraschend auf ein neugotisches Pfarrhaus trifft, das seit ewigen Zeiten am Rand eines Dorfes steht, neben einer inzwischen baufälligen Kirche und einem

John Constable,
*Malvern Hall,
Warwickshire* (1809),
Tate Gallery, London

LES MAISONS ROMANTIQUES D'ANGLETERRE

En évoquant la beauté rurale de l'Angleterre, on est assiégé par des images inoubliables, car ce qui reste gravé pour toujours dans notre mémoire, c'est la première confrontation avec les paysages ondulants – immortalisés par Gainsborough, Turner ou Constable – où le vent impitoyable lutte contre les arbres noueux et leurs branches tordues et qui semblent courber le dos sous un ciel lourd de nuages. Se rappeler le charme pastoral de l'Angleterre, c'est se souvenir du jour où l'on s'est trouvé face à une imposante demeure palladienne, perdue au milieu d'un immense parc peuplé de statues et de folies, et c'est subir le choc visuel causé par un modeste cottage couronné de chaume dont la silhouette se mire dans une rivière sinueuse aux reflets d'argent.

Qui dit Angleterre dit campagne et, dans ces contrées verdoyantes, il n'est pas rare de croiser un manoir du 18e siècle dans le plus pur style georgien ou de se laisser surprendre par un vieux presbytère aux allures gothiques, planté il y a des siècles à la sortie d'un village doté d'une église vétuste et d'un petit cimetière aux pierres tombales couvertes de mousse. On trouvera ici un repos bien mérité dans un pub lambrissé de chêne qui vous promet les délices d'une bonne bière blonde et d'un «shepherd's pie» brûlant!

Parcourir le pays de Jane Austen, de Shakespeare et de Thomas Hardy, c'est fredonner les paroles gonflées de nostalgie d'une vieille chanson:

John Constable,
*Flatford Mill · Die
Flatford-Mühle ·
Le Moulin de Flatford*
(1817), Tate Gallery,
London

All this amounts to something more than mere cliché, for the English themselves expect it. The fact is that the land of Jane Austen, Shakespeare and Thomas Hardy brims with unforced nostalgia. When English people sing the sentimental music-hall song:

"There'll always be an England,

While there's a country lane,

Wherever there's a cottage small,

Beside a field of grain."

they are repeating a mantra that has lost nothing of its emotional potency. Again, their most hackneyed proverb – "An Englishman's home is his castle" – articulates not so much a point of law as a deep yearning.

In "Jane Eyre" the novelist Charlotte Brontë describes just such a yearning: "My home then – when I at last find a home – is a cottage: a little room with white-washed walls, and a sanded floor; containing four painted chairs and a table, a clock, a cupboard, with two or three plates and dishes, and a set of tea things in Delft. Above, a chamber of the same dimensions as the kitchen, with a deal bedstead, and a chest of drawers; small, yet too large to be filled with my scanty wardrobe". In spite of their age and the passing of the era in which they were written, Brontë's words perfectly express the unquenchable passion of her countrymen for the ordinary charms of their rural provinces.

Another curious feature of the English countryside is the almost daily sense of "déjà vu" it seems to induce. So much in these sleepy places – the thatched roofs, the narrow lace-curtained windows, the walls foaming with roses – seems intensely familiar. Miss Marple is surely to be found here, taking tea with a friend, on the trail of a murderer. It is all too easy to imagine that the tall figure of a woman

kleinen Friedhof mit moosbewachsenen Grabsteinen. In einem eichengetäfelten Pub legt man dann eine wohlverdiente Rast ein, genießt ein Ale und einen glühendheißen »Shepherd's Pie« …

Diese Bilder sind nicht nur Klischees; auch die Engländer sehen sich und ihr Land auf diese Weise. Durch das Land von Jane Austen, Shakespeare und Thomas Hardy zu reisen heißt, die Melodie eines nostalgischen, alten Liedes mitzusummen:
> »There'll always be an England,
> While there's a country lane,
> Wherever there's a cottage small,
> Beside a field of grain.«

Diese Zeilen stimmen auch heute noch sentimental und beweisen die zeitlose Gültigkeit der englischen Redensart »An Englishman's home is his castle«.

In »Jane Eyre« schrieb die Autorin Charlotte Brontë: »Mein Heim – wenn ich endlich ein Heim finde, wird ein kleines Cottage sein: ein kleines Zimmer mit weiß getünchten Wänden und Sandfußboden. Mit vier lackierten Stühlen und einem Tisch, einer Uhr, einer Anrichte mit einigen Tellern und Schüsseln und einem Teeservice aus Delfter Fayence. In der Etage darüber eine Kammer in der gleichen Größe wie die Küche, mit einem Bett aus Fichte und einer Kommode, klein und doch zu groß, um meine bescheidene Garderobe aufzu-

John Constable, *Parham Mill, Gillingham · Die Parham-Mühle, Gillingham · Le Moulin de Parham, Gillingham* (1826), Yale Center for British Art, New Haven, Connecticut

> «There'll always be an England,
> While there's a country lane,
> Wherever there's a cottage small,
> Beside a field of grain.»

Cette chanson n'a rien perdu de sa valeur sentimentale et prouve aussi que le dicton anglais «An Englishman's home is his castle» renferme une vérité inébranlable.

Dans «Jane Eyre», la romancière Charlotte Brontë écrit: «Ma maison, puisque j'ai enfin trouvé une maison, est un cottage; une petite pièce aux murs blanchis à la chaux, au sol recouvert de sable, contenant quatre chaises peintes, une table, une horloge, un bahut garni de deux ou trois assiettes, de plats, et d'un service à thé en faïence de Delft. Au-dessus, une chambre de même dimension que la cuisine, avec un lit en bois blanc, et une petite commode, encore trop grande pour être remplie par ma garde-robe sommaire…» En dépit de leur grand âge et de l'époque à laquelle ils furent écrits, ces mots illustrent parfaitement la passion qu'éprouvent les Anglais pour les charmes modestes de leur «countryside».

Et puis, ce qui nous attire particulièrement dans la campagne anglaise, c'est l'expérience du «déjà-vu». En effet, tout nous semble familier dans ce village somnolant où se dressent des maisons couvertes de rosiers grimpants, aux toits de chaume et aux petites fenêtres garnies de rideaux de dentelle. On s'y représente une Miss Marple en herbe, avide de meurtre, rece-

John Constable, *The Valley Farm · Bauernhof im Tal · La Ferme dans la vallée* (1835), Tate Gallery, London

Thomas Gains-
borough, *The Painter's
Daughters with a Cat
(unfinished)* · *Die
Töchter des Künstlers
mit einer Katze
(unvollendet)* ·
*Les Filles du peintre
tenant un chat
(inachevé)*,
(1758–1760),
National Gallery,
London

LEFT · LINKS ·
A GAUCHE: Detail of
a painting by Thomas
Gainsborough,
*The Honourable Mrs.
Graham* (1775–1777),
National Gallery of
Scotland, Edinburgh

glimpsed at the turn of a muddy track might be Thomas Hardy's Tess of the D'Urbervilles or that the gentleman at the wheel of some elderly Bentley waiting in front of a parsonage is none other than P. G. Wodehouse's immaculate Jeeves.

There is mystery, too. It springs from generations of stories told on winter evenings around rural firesides; tales of black-garbed ladies wandering by night through the passages of old buildings, of stifled sobs and sighs and footfalls half-heard in the attics of abandoned farmhouses. Ghosts, it seems, are firmly established among the special rural privileges and assets of England, about which even Jonathan Swift – that scourge of English humbug – was moved to write the following lines:

"I often wished that I had clear,
For life, six hundred pounds a year,
A handsome house to lodge a friend,
A river at my garden's end,
A terrace walk, and half a rood
Of land, set out to plant a wood."

Humanity's love of the countryside is ageless and universal. But in England above all other places that love remains a potent, living force.

nehmen«. Trotz ihres beträchtlichen Alters illustrieren diese Worte heute immer noch die heimliche Liebe der Engländer für den schlichten Charme ihrer »Countryside«.

Besonders das geheimnisvolle Flair der englischen Landschaft hat es uns angetan. Genährt wird es von alten Legenden, die an Winterabenden am Kaminfeuer erzählt werden. Angenehm schaudern wir bei den Geschichten von Gespenstern, von der »Dame in Schwarz«, die nachts durch die Flure eines alten Herrenhauses irrt, oder den Schreien, Seufzern und Schritten, die angeblich auf dem Speicher des alten, verlassenen Bauernhofs zu hören sind. Gespenster und Geister sind das Privileg dieser Insel, die auch Jonathan Swift zu romantischen Versen inspirierte:

> »Ich wünschte oft, ich hätte bar
> Ein Leben lang sechshundert Pfund pro Jahr,
> Ein hübsches Haus und guten Freund bei mir,
> Ein Flüßchen am Gartenrand dann hier,
> Eine Terrasse und einen Acker Boden,
> Den würde ich für einen Wald dann roden.«

Die Liebe zum Landleben hat es zu allen Zeiten gegeben. Doch nirgendwo ist sie stärker und gegenwärtiger als in England…

Thomas Gainsborough, *The Artist's Daughter Mary · Bildnis der Tochter Mary · Mary, la fille du peintre* (1777), Tate Gallery, London

Thomas Gainsborough, *Mrs. Richard Brinsley Sheridan* (1785–1786), National Gallery, Paul Mellon Collection, Washington D. C.

FOLLOWING PAGES · FOLGENDE DOPPELSEITE · DOUBLE PAGE SUIVANTE: John Constable, *Cloud Study · Stratokumulus-Wolken · Etude de nuage* (1821), Yale Center for British Art, Paul Mellon Collection, New Haven, Connecticut

vant ses amies pour le thé et pour les commérages. De toute façon, il faut si peu pour que l'imagination s'enflamme et pour que nous pensions reconnaître, au détour d'un chemin boueux, la silhouette élancée de Tess d'Urberville, ou l'exquis Jeeves, imaginé par P.G. Wodehouse, immobile derrière le volant de la vieille Bentley garée devant le presbytère.

Décidément l'Angleterre nous abreuve d'illusions et de mystères et elle ne tarit pas de vieilles légendes racontées un soir d'hiver au coin du feu, d'histoires de fantômes provoquant des frissons délicieux; elle nous parle de démons et de «la dame en noir» qui rôde la nuit dans les couloirs du vieux manoir, de soupirs et de pas qui résonnent – dit-on – dans le grenier de la grande ferme abandonnée. Ils sont le privilège de cette île apparemment hantée dans laquelle Jonathan Swift, dans «Invitation of Horace», en 1714 rêvait ces vers imprégnés de romantisme:

> «J'ai souvent désiré avoir ma foi
> six cents livres de rente pour la vie,
> Une belle maison où loger un ami,
> Avec une rivière au bout du jardin,
> Un chemin en terrasse et un lopin
> De terre, assez pour y planter un bois.»

L'amour de la campagne est de tous les temps. Mais c'est en Angleterre que nous le percevons dans sa forme la plus puissante…

CHAWTON COTTAGE
Jane Austen

Hampshire

Dusk was falling when Jane Austen and her mother arrived in Alton. It was 7 July 1809, and the two had come by coach to settle in the modest cottage lent to them by Jane's brother Edward, a wealthy banker. Jane was frail, hypersensitive and worn out by the many moves her family had made since her childhood in the vicarage at Steventon. At 33 years old, she had already written two masterpieces – "Sense and Sensibility" and "Pride and Prejudice"– and she dreamed of finding at Chawton the peace and repose she so badly needed to remain creative and productive. And so it proved. For nine years thereafter – until her untimely death at Winchester in 1817 – Chawton was to be Jane's haven of quiet, where she spent the days working at her table by the window, completing her great novels, "Mansfield Park", "Emma", and "Persuasion". Jane's time was spent writing, playing the piano or helping her mother, her devoted sister Cassandra, and their friend Martha Lloyd with domestic chores; her only social diversions were afternoon tea and an occasional dinner with friends. Today, visitors from all over the world make the pilgrimage to Chawton Cottage, which is now a museum. Nothing has changed in the little house: the dining room table with its Wedgwood service seems to await the arrival of guests, the little desk is in its place, and the shade of Jane herself still seems to hover in the passages.

ABOVE: *the Gothic window embrasure in the drawing-room wall.*
LEFT: *a blue and white bowl and pitcher dating from the 19th century.*

OBEN: *Das Fenster im neugotischen Stil wurde nachträglich in die Mauer des Salons eingesetzt.*
LINKS: *eine Waschgarnitur mit blau-weißem Dekor aus dem 19. Jahrhundert.*

CI-DESSUS: *la fenêtre de style gothique découpée dans le mur du salon.*
A GAUCHE: *un pot de chambre à décor bleu et blanc datant du 19ᵉ siècle.*

Es dämmerte schon, als Jane Austen mit ihrer Mutter am 7. Juli 1809 mit der Postkutsche in Alton eintraf, um das kleine Cottage zu beziehen, das ihr Bruder Edward, ein wohlhabender Bankier, ihnen zur Verfügung gestellt hatte. Die zarte Jane war zermürbt von den vielen Umzügen, die sie seit ihrer Geburt im Pfarrhaus von Steventon im Jahr 1775 erlebt hatte. Nun war sie 33 Jahre alt und hatte bereits die beiden Romane »Gefühl und Verstand« sowie »Stolz und Vorurteil« geschrieben. Sie hoffte, endlich die für ihre Kreativität so wichtige Ruhe zu finden. In den folgenden neun Jahren, bis zu ihrem frühen Tod in Winchester im Jahr 1817, wurde Chawton Cottage für die Schriftstellerin zu einer Oase der Ruhe. Ihre Tage verbrachte sie damit, ihre Meisterwerke »Mansfield Park«, »Emma« und »Anne Elliot« an einem kleinen Tisch im Speisezimmer zu schreiben, auf dem Klavier im Salon zu spielen, oder ihrer Mutter, ihrer Schwester Cassandra und der gemeinsamen Freundin Martha Lloyd im Haushalt zu helfen. Das Leben verlief friedlich und wurde allenfalls vom »Afternoon Tea« oder einem Dinner mit Freunden unterbrochen. Besucher finden heute in Chawton Cottage, das inzwischen ein Museum ist, noch die Atmosphäre von damals vor: Der Eßtisch ist mit Wedgwood-Geschirr gedeckt, der kleine Tisch steht nach wie vor an seinem Platz.

Portraits of Jane Austen are very rare, and only a few likenesses now exist.

Es existieren nur einige wenige Porträts von Jane Austen, die ihr auch wirklich ähnlich sehen.

Très peu de portraits ressemblants de Jane Austen nous sommes parvenus et les quelques exemples existants se font rares.

In the time of Jane Austen, the garden surrounding Chawton Cottage was much larger.

Zu Lebzeiten von Jane Austen war der Garten von Chawton Cottage wesentlich größer.

Du temps de Jane Austen, le jardin qui entoure Chawton Cottage était beaucoup plus vaste.

Le soir tombait lorsque Jane Austen et sa mère arrivèrent en diligence à Alton dans le Hampshire, le 7 juillet 1809, pour s'installer dans le modeste cottage que son frère Edward, un richissime banquier, avait mis gentiment à leur disposition. Jane, frêle, hypersensible et épuisée par les nombreux déménagements qu'elle avait dû subir depuis sa naissance en 1775 dans le presbytère de Steventon, avait 33 ans, et n'ayant à cette date écrit que deux romans, «Raison et sentiments» et «Orgueil et préjugés», elle rêvait de trouver à Chawton Cottage le repos si nécessaire à l'inspiration. Pendant neuf ans – jusqu'à sa mort prématurée à Winchester en 1817 – l'écrivain allait trouver ici un havre de paix, passant ses jours à écrire ses incontestables chefs-d'œuvre «Mansfield Park», «Emma» et «Persuasion» sur un petit guéridon près de la fenêtre de la salle à manger, jouant du pianoforte dans le salon, ou aidant sa mère, sa sœur dévouée Cassandra et leur amie commune Martha Lloyd, dans les travaux du ménage, voyant sa vie paisible à peine interrompue par un «afternoon tea» ou un dîner avec des amis. Les visiteurs qui viennent du monde entier à Chawton Cottage – aujourd'hui transformé en musée – y trouvent toujours l'ambiance d'antan. La table dressée et parée d'un service de Wedgwood semble attendre les invités, le petit guéridon est toujours à sa place et le fantôme de Jane semble rôder dans les couloirs…

LEFT: *Today, the old bakehouse, granary and well look much as they originally did, largely due to careful and intelligent restoration.*

FACING PAGE: *In the bakehouse, the bread oven, the vat and a beehive seem to await the energetic Mrs Austen, Jane's mother, who was a gifted gardener and a housekeeper second to none.*

LINKS: *Die alte Backstube, die Kornkammer und der Brunnen besitzen heute dank sorgfältiger Restaurierung wieder ihren originalen Charakter.*

RECHTE SEITE: *In der alten Backstube scheinen der Backofen, der Waschzuber und ein hölzerner Bienenstock auf die energische Mrs. Austen zu warten. Janes Mutter war eine ausgezeichnete Hausfrau und begabte Gärtnerin…*

A GAUCHE: *Le vieux fournil, la grange à blé et le puits ont gardé leur aspect d'antan grâce à une restauration méticuleuse et intelligente.*

PAGE DE DROITE: *Dans le fournil, le four à pain, le cuvier et une ruche en bois semblent attendre l'arrivée de l'énergique Mrs. Austen. La mère de Jane était une excellente ménagère et jardinière de talent…*

LEFT: *The copper kettle could have been used by Jane to make tea. Among other things, she was in charge of preparing breakfast and kept the key to the cupboard where the tea and coffee were stored.*
FACING PAGE: *the pedestal table at which Jane wrote several of her famous novels, with one of her letters and her simple inkwell.*

LINKS: *Den kupfernen Teekessel hat Jane vielleicht für die Zubereitung von Tee verwendet. Sie war für das tägliche »Breakfast« zuständig und besaß den Schlüssel zur Vorratskammer mit Tee und Kaffee.*
RECHTE SEITE: *Der kleine Tisch, an dem Jane mehrere ihrer berühmten Romane schrieb, dient heute als Ablage für das schlichte Tintenfaß und einen Brief der Schriftstellerin.*

A GAUCHE: *Jane aurait pu se servir de la bouilloire en cuivre pour faire du thé, car c'est elle qui préparait le «breakfast» quotidien et qui possédait la clef du placard où l'on gardait le thé et le café.*
PAGE DE DROITE: *Sur le guéridon où Jane écrivit plusieurs de ses célèbres romans, on découvre une lettre de l'écrivain et son modeste encrier.*

"The folly of people's not staying comfortably at home when they can! … five dull hours in another man's house, … four horses and four servants taken out for nothing but to convey five idle shivering creatures into colder rooms and worse company than they might have had at home."

»Wie töricht doch die Menschen sind, nicht nach Möglichkeit zuhause zu bleiben! … fünf öde Stunden im Haus anderer Leute, … vier Pferde und vier Bedienstete werden nur geweckt, um fünf müßige bibbernde Kreaturen in ein noch kühleres Zimmer mit noch schlechterer Gesellschaft zu führen, als sie zuhause gehabt hätten.«

«Bien fous ceux qui ne restent pas confortablement chez eux quand ils le peuvent!… Cinq heures maussades passées dans la maison d'autrui… quatre chevaux et quatre domestiques ne servant à rien qu'à amener cinq pauvres créatures grelottantes et désœuvrées dans des pièces glacées où elles se retrouvent en plus mauvaise compagnie que chez elles.»

JANE AUSTEN
Emma

FACING PAGE: *in the dining parlour, a neo-classical fireplace, flowered wallpaper and the framed silhouettes of Mrs Austen and Cassandra – all perfectly reflecting the contemporary taste for restraint in decoration.*
RIGHT: *A full-length portrait of Jane's third brother, Edward Austen Knight, graces the rear wall of the dining parlour. Jane was particularly fond of the Wedgwood service.*

LINKE SEITE: *Im Eßzimmer spiegeln der neoklassizistische Kamin, die Blumenta-pete und die gerahmten Scherenschnitte von Mrs. Austen und Cassandra perfekt den damaligen puritani-schen Einrichtungsstil wider.*
RECHTS: *Ein ganz-figuriges Porträt von Janes drittem Bruder Edward Austen Knight ziert die hintere Wand des Speisezimmers. Jane schätzte das Wedgwood-Geschirr ganz besonders.*

PAGE DE GAUCHE: *Dans la salle à manger, une cheminée néoclas-sique, un papier peint à fleurs et les profils enca-drés de Mrs. Austen et de Cassandra reflètent parfaitement le goût de l'époque pour une déco-ration dépouillée.*
A DROITE: *Un portrait en pied du troisième frère de Jane, Edward Austen Knight, orne le mur du fond du «dining parlour». Jane était particulièrement éprise du service Wedgwood.*

LEFT: *The hallway, with one of the late 18th-century Hepplewhite chairs that formerly belonged to Jane's father, George Austen, and was transported all the way to Chawton Cottage from the rectory at Steventon.*

LINKS: *Im Flur steht einer der Stühle im Hepplewhitestil aus dem späten 18. Jahrhundert, die noch von Janes Vater George Austen stammen und den weiten Weg vom Pfarrhaus in Steventon bis nach Chawton Cottage zurückgelegt haben.*

A GAUCHE: *Le vestibule avec un des sièges Hepplewhite de la fin du 18ᵉ siècle qui appartenaient au père de Jane, George Austen, et qui firent un long voyage entre le presbytère de Steventon et Chawton Cottage.*

RIGHT: *In one of the bedrooms on the first floor, a Regency chair, a Georgian looking glass and a built-in wardrobe transform what was otherwise a tiny bedroom into a comfortable dressing room*
FACING PAGE: *the view from the hallway through to the dining-parlour. The dining-room table was borrowed by Jane from her brother Edward, and one can well imagine the Austen family assembled around a similar table, relishing a pigeon pie.*

RECHTS: *Ein Regency-Stuhl, ein georgianischer Spiegel und ein Einbauschrank verwandeln ein winziges Schlafzimmer in der ersten Etage in ein gemütliches Ankleidezimmer.*

RECHTE SEITE: *die Diele mit Blick ins Speisezimmer. Den Eßtisch hatte sich Jane von ihrem Bruder Edward ausgeliehen. Man kann sich ohne weiteres vorstellen, wie die Familie Austen am Tisch bei einem »Pigeon Pie« sitzt.*

A DROITE: *Dans une des chambres à l'étage, une chaise Regency, un miroir georgien et une armoire encastrée transform une minuscule chambre à coucher en dressing-room confortable.*
PAGE DE DROITE: *Du vestibule on a une très jolie vue sur la salle à manger. La table de la salle à manger fut empruntée par Jane à son frère Edward. On peut s'imaginer la famille Austen réunie autour d'une grande table en train de se régaler d'un «pigeon pie».*

A GEORGIAN HOUSE
Jill and Lincoln Cato

Sussex

The Catos' house is close to the seashore and one surmises that it
dates from the building craze that hit the quiet little town of
Brighton in the early years of the 19th century as a result of the
Royal Pavilion project initiated by the Prince Regent (future George
IV). What sets it apart from its contemporary neighbours is a clear
lack of pretension and pomposity. It is a simple Georgian house
with a plain white front, no more and no less. The cabinetmaker
Lincoln Cato and his wife, who bought the place four years ago,
claim they fell in love with its many internal shutters. In their work,
the Catos are ready to tackle anything in the field of restoration, but
oddly enough their real preference is for antiques that have not been
restored. They also like venerable patinas and flaky oil paintings,
and as a result their interior is filled with pretty 18th-century furniture scrubbed white, stags' antlers, late 18th-century Gustavian
chairs in their original condition and treasures brought back from
the beach. The overall impression is that their house has not been
meddled with in years. Add to this an expanse of fine silver-sheened
wooden flooring, a custard-coloured kitchen with a pair of weighty
pine sideboards, and a drawing room stuffed with neoclassical furniture and objects – and the picture of subdued elegance is complete.

*A 19th-century biscuit
statuette of Gallic fight-
ers stands on a Regency
bench reproduced by
Cato.*

*Auf einer von Cato an-
gefertigten Kopie einer
Regency-Bank steht
eine Statuette aus
Biskuitporzellan aus
dem 19. Jahrhundert,
die kämpfende Gallier
darstellt.*

*Un statuette en biscuit
19ᵉ représentant des
gaulois luttant est posée
sur une banquette
Regency réédité par
Cato.*

Das Haus der Catos liegt direkt am Meer, und man kann sich gut vorstellen, daß es zur Zeit des Prinzregenten, des zukünftigen George IV., errichtet wurde, der mit seinem märchenhaften Royal Pavilion in der ruhigen Küstenstadt Brighton zu Beginn des 19. Jahrhunderts eine regelrechte Bauwut ausgelöst hatte. Jedoch unterscheidet sich das einfache georgianische Haus mit der schmucklosen weißen Fassade von den anderen Gebäuden aus dieser Zeit, denn es ist weder prätentiös noch pompös. Vor vier Jahren verliebten sich der Kunstschreiner Lincoln Cato und seine Frau Jill vor allem wegen der vielen Fensterläden im Innern in das Haus. Sie sind zwar beruflich äußerst versierte Restauratoren, doch sie schätzen auch die Patina von nicht restaurierten Antiquitäten und Gemälde mit abblätternder Farbe. Ihr Haus haben sie mit hübschen Möbeln aus dem 18. Jahrhundert eingerichtet, die mit Lauge gebleicht wurden. Überall finden sich Geweihe, Stühle im »Gustavian-Style« aus dem späten 18. Jahrhundert und »Schätze«, die die Catos am Strand aufgelesen haben. Das Ambiente wirkt, als sei es seit Ewigkeiten unberührt. Die silbrig glänzenden Holzbohlen, die in sattem Karamelton gestrichene Küche mit einem Paar schwergewichtiger Anrichten aus Kiefer sowie das Wohnzimmer mit zahlreichen neoklassizistischen Möbeln und Objekten machen den optischen Genuß perfekt…

The Catos have a manifest passion for antlers, which are hung all over the house. Antlers adorn the stucco column which stands on the dining-room mantel.

Die Catos begeistern sich für Geweihe, die sich im ganzen Haus finden – sogar auf der Gipssäule auf dem Kaminsims im Eßzimmer.

Les Cato ont une passion pour les bois de cerf – ils sont partout dans la maison! Sur la cheminée de la salle à manger, ils ornent une colonne en stuc.

La maison se trouve à deux pas de la mer et on peut imaginer qu'à l'époque du Prince Régent, futur George IV, et de son féerique Royal Pavilion, elle vit le jour pendant la folie de la construction qui frappa sans pitié cette petite ville côtière tranquille au début du 19ᵉ siècle. Ce qui la distingue des autres bâtiments, c'est qu'elle n'a rien de prétentieux ni de grandiose. C'est une simple maison de style georgien avec une façade blanche dépourvue d'ornements inutiles, et l'ébéniste Lincoln Cato et sa femme Jill qui l'achetèrent il y a quatre ans, prétendent qu'ils s'éprirent des lieux à cause de la présence des nombreux volets intérieurs. Depuis lors, les Lincoln ont prouvé que – côté restauration – ils n'ont pas froid aux yeux, mais comme ils préfèrent les antiquités non restaurées, les patines anciennes, et même les peintures écaillées, leur intérieur rempli de jolis meubles 18ᵉ blanchis par le récurage à l'eau javellisée, de bois de cerf omniprésents, de sièges gustaviens de la fin du 18ᵉ siècle et de «trésors» ramenés de la plage, donne l'impression de ne pas avoir été touché depuis une éternité. Ajoutons-y la présence de très beaux planchers à reflets d'argent, d'une cuisine couleur «crème caramel» équipée d'une paire de grands buffets en pin et d'un séjour bourré de meubles et d'objets néoclassiques, et l'image du bonheur esthétique est parfaite…

True to 19th-century tradition, the Catos heat their house with coal.

Die Catos heizen ihr Haus auch im Stil des 19. Jahrhunderts: mit Kohle.

Fidèles aux traditions du 19ᵉ siècle, les Cato chauffent leur maison au charbon.

LEFT: *In the entrance, the whitened skull of an animal seems to stare at a still life made from a strip of bark, a horse-shoe, moss, branches and shells. The chest of drawers and the obeliskis are by Lincoln Cato.*

LINKS: *Der ausge-blichene Tierschädel in der Eingangshalle scheint aufmerksam ein Stilleben aus Holzrinde, Hufeisen, Moos, Zwei-gen und Muscheln zu begutachten. Die Kommode und die Obelisken sind Werke von Lincoln Cato.*

A GAUCHE: *Dans l'en-trée, un crâne d'animal blanchi semble observer intensément la nature morte composée d'un fragment d'écorce, d'un fer à cheval et d'un coussin de mousse, de branches et de coquilles. La commode et les obé-lisques sont signés Lin-coln Cato.*

RECHTS: *Das Haus von Jill und Lincoln ist kein Museum: Die Söh-ne verstauen ihre Bälle in einer neoklassizisti-schen gußeisernen Urne aus dem 19. Jahrhun-dert.*

RECHTE SEITE: *Im Eßzimmer umgeben Hirschgeweihe den Tisch mit den Stühlen im »Gustavian-Style«. Die Buchstaben über der Tür stammen aus einem Restaurant.*

A DROITE: *La maison de Jill et Lincoln n'est pas un musée stérile et leurs fils gardent les balles de «soccer» dans une urne néoclassique en fonte du 19e siècle.*

PAGE DE DROITE: *Dans la salle à manger, les incontournables bois de cerf entourent la table et les chaises gusta-viennes. Les lettres au-dessus de la porte pro-viennent d'un restaurant.*

RIGHT: *The Catos' house is no museum; their sons keep their footballs in a neoclassi-cal cast-iron urn made in the 19th century.*
FACING PAGE: *More antlers surround the table and the Gustavian chairs. The letters above the door come from a restaurant.*

Period 18th-century
Swedish chairs and
copies from Ikea coexist
peacefully around the
gateleg table, which has
been bleached by repeat-
ed scrubbings with soda.
The desk is one of Lin-
coln's creations, inspired
by a Biedermeier origi-
nal.

Schwedische Stühle aus
dem 18. Jahrhundert
stehen friedlich neben
Nachbauten von Ikea
an einem mit Chlor-
wasser gebleichten Gate-
leg table. Lincoln hat
den Sekretär nach
einem Vorbild aus dem
Biedermeier angefertigt.

Des chaises suédoises 18ᵉ
et des copies de chez
Ikéa cohabitent paisi-
blement autour de la
table «gateleg» blanchie
par un lavage fréquent
à l'eau javellisée. Le
meuble secrétaire est une
création de Lincoln et
s'inspire d'un modèle
Biedermeier.

ABOVE: *On either side of the old gas cooker, Lincoln has installed practical cupboards made of pitch pine.*
RIGHT: *An 18th-century chair, an old kitchen table and floorboards washed down with water reflect the Catos' taste for light-coloured, matwood surfaces.*
FACING PAGE: *In the first-floor living room, the style is Georgian. The fireplace and its Adam-style fender date from the late 18th century, but the baroque looking glass and the sofa are both recent creations by Lincoln Cato.*

OBEN: *Auf beiden Seiten des Gasherdes hat Lincoln praktische Schränke aus Pechkiefer aufgestellt.*
RECHTS: *Ein Stuhl aus dem 18. Jahrhundert, ein alter Küchentisch und ausgewaschene Holzbohlen zeugen von Jills und Lincolns Vorliebe für mattes, helles Holz.*
RECHTE SEITE: *Der Salon auf der ersten Etage ist im georgianischen Stil gehalten. Der Kamin mit dem Gitter stammt aus dem späten 18. Jahrhundert, aber der »barocke« Spiegel und das Canapé sind neuere Werke von Lincoln.*

CI-DESSUS: *De part et d'autre de l'ancienne cuisinière à gaz, Lincoln a installé des armoires pratiques en pitchpin.*
A DROITE: *Une chaise 18e, une ancienne table de cuisine et un plancher lavés à l'eau, révèlent la prédilection de Jill et Lincoln pour un bois clair et mat.*
PAGE DE DROITE: *Dans le salon du premier étage, le ton est au style georgien. La cheminée et sa grille de style Adam – style élégant du 18e siécle tardif – sont d'époque, mais le miroir «baroque» et le canapé sont des créations récentes de Lincoln.*

JACOBEAN HOUSE

Wiltshire

The Swedish decorator Filippa Naess loves England, English style and the English countryside, but she especially loves old manor houses in which each item of furniture carries an imprint of the past. She lives in London, where international clients come to seek her advice on how to create warm, comfortable, and welcoming interiors. The clients who asked her to decorate their manor house in Wiltshire – a stout early 17th-century building in the very purest Jacobean tradition – knew all about Filippa's predilection for old velvets, four-poster beds, Tuscan ochre, terracotta pigments, and the discreet glimmer of old gold. The very existence of their house was a jealously-guarded secret; what they wanted for it was the kind of ambiance that would reflect their taste for fine period furniture, dark polished wood, precious carpets and voluminous drapes like the ones in the paintings of 17th-century masters. The result is a resounding success on all counts, and today Filippa's subtle interplays of colour, combined with an excellent collection of antique furniture and the decorative effect of works by the great names of contemporary art, combine to make this old manor a place of beauty and comfort.

A stone torso placed on a robust antique table catches the light shining through one of the leaded glass windows.

Ein steinerner Torso auf einem soliden antiken Tisch fängt das Licht, das durch eines der bleiverglasten Fenster eindringt.

Un torse en pierre placé sur une solide table ancienne capte parfaitement la lumière qui entre par une des fenêtres à vitraux.

A circular aperture in the old wall surrounding the garden offers a magnificent view across the lawn to the trees and clipped hedges.

Die runde Öffnung in der alten Gartenmauer gewährt einen herrlichen Blick auf den Garten mit seinen beschnittenen Hecken.

Dans le vieux mur qui entoure le jardin, une ouverture circulaire offre une vue magnifique sur la pelouse et sur les arbres et les haies taillées.

Die schwedische Dekorateurin Filippa Naess liebt England, den englischen Wohnstil, die englische Landschaft und die alten Herrenhäuser, in denen jedes einzelne Möbelstück und Objekt von der Vergangenheit zeugt. Deshalb lebt sie in London, wo sie für ihre internationale Klientel besonders gemütliche und einladende Räume entwirft. Die Kunden, die sie baten, ihr Herrenhaus in Wiltshire einzurichten – ein ehrwürdiges Gebäude aus dem frühen 17. Jahrhundert im reinen »Jacobean-Style« – kannten Filippas Vorliebe für schwere alte Samtstoffe, für Himmelbetten, die Farbe Ocker, toskanische Terrakotta und den besonderen Charme von altem Gold. Als sie ihr die Einrichtung ihres Hauses anvertrauten, das sie bewußt geheim halten, wollten sie einen angemessenen Rahmen schaffen für ihre erlesenen antiken Möbel, dunklen, gut gewachsten Hölzer, kostbaren Teppiche und Stoffe, die so großzügig wie auf den Gemälden des 17. Jahrhunderts drapiert wurden. Filippa konnte diesen Wunsch voll und ganz befriedigen. Heute besticht das alte Herrenhaus durch das subtile Spiel mit schillernden Farben sowie durch die bemerkenswerte Sammlung antiker Möbel und Originalwerke von bekannten zeitgenössischen Künstlern.

La décoratrice suédoise Filippa Naess adore l'Angleterre, le style «british», la campagne anglaise et les vieux manoirs où chaque meuble et chaque objet porte l'empreinte du passé. Elle a choisi de vivre à Londres où une clientèle international vient lui demander aide et conseil pour créer des intérieurs qui se distinguent par le souci du confort et par une ambiance chaleureuse et accueillante. Les clients qui lui demandèrent de s'occuper de leur manoir dans le Wiltshire – une vénérable bâtisse érigée dans le plus pur style jacobéen du début du 17e siècle – connaissaient la prédilection de Filippa pour les velours anciens, les ocres et les terre cuites de Toscane, l'éclat discret du vieil or et les lits à baldaquin. En lui confiant la décoration intérieure de cette maison dont ils gardent jalousement le secret, ils s'assuraient d'une ambiance qui serait l'écho de leur goût prononcé pour les meubles de haute époque, les bois sombres bien cirés, les tapis précieux et les tissus généreusement drapés tels qu'on les découvre sur les tableaux des maîtres du 17e siècle. Filippa a pleinement réussi à satisfaire tous leurs désirs et, aujourd'hui, son jeu subtil de couleurs chatoyantes, la présence d'une collection de meubles anciens d'une qualité remarquable, et l'apport décoratif d'œuvres signées par les grands noms de l'art contemporain, transforment le vieux manoir en un havre de beauté et de bien-être.

An ancient stone bench, gently curved, waits enticingly just outside the broad drawing-room window.

Vor dem Fenster zum Salon lädt eine alte, leicht gebogene Bank aus Stein zum Verweilen ein.

Un ancien banc en pierre légèrement arrondi, installé devant la grande fenêtre qui donne sur le «drawing room», invite le promeneur au repos.

FACING PAGE: *A 17th-century lantern and a table from the same period echo the sober décor. The print is by Henry Moore (1898–1986).*
ABOVE: *A marble head dating from Roman times, a spectacular baroque mirror and a 17th-century bronze candelabra add a note of luxury to this deliberately austere composition.*
RIGHT: *In one of the passages, Filippa has enriched the minimalist architecture with richly-dyed rugs and Jacobean chairs covered with bright blue velvet.*

LINKE SEITE: *Eine Laterne und ein Tisch aus dem 17. Jahrhundert gehören zu der spartanischen Einrichtung. Die Lithographie stammt von Henry Moore (1898–1986).*
OBEN: *Ein römischer Marmorkopf, ein barocker Spiegel und ein bronzener Kerzenständer aus dem 17. Jahrhundert geben der bewußt strengen Anordnung eine luxuriöse Note.*
RECHTS: *In einem der Flure hat Filippa die schlichte Architektur mit bunten Teppichen und Stühlen im »Jacobean-Style« aufgelockert.*

PAGE DE GAUCHE: *Une lanterne et une table, toutes deux du 17ᵉ siècle, font écho à ce décor sobre. La lithographie est signée Henry Moore (1898–1986).*
CI-DESSUS: *Une tête en marbre d'époque romaine, un miroir baroque et un candélabre en bronze 17ᵉ ajoutent une note luxueuse à cette composition austère.*
A DROITE: *Dans un des corridors, Filippa a enrichi l'architecture minimaliste de tapis aux couleurs vives et de chaises jacobéennes dont l'assise est recouverte de velours bleu roi.*

LEFT: *In the dining room, the majestic hearth and the robust Jacobean furniture speak to us of the era of Shakespeare and Marlowe, when good things and good cheer were appreciated to the full.*
FACING PAGE: *Even if it is an otherwise perfect imitation of a period kitchen, with a fireplace several centuries old, no English kitchen is considered complete without an Aga.*

LINKS: *Im Eßzimmer lassen der majestätische Kamin und die robusten Möbel die längst vergangene Ära von Shakespeare und Marlowe aufleben, als man Wohlbefinden und Gastlichkeit zu schätzen wußte…*
RECHTE SEITE: *Diese englische Küche ist ein vollendetes Ebenbild der Küchen von einst. Obwohl sie über einen mehrere Jahrhunderte alten Kamin verfügt, wäre sie doch nicht perfekt ohne den alten Herd der Firma Aga!*

A GAUCHE: *Dans la salle à manger, l'âtre majestueux et le robuste mobilier jacobéen nous parlent d'une époque lointaine, contemporaine de Shakespeare et de Marlowe, où le bienêtre et la bonne chère étaient fort appréciés…*
PAGE DE DROITE: *Une cuisine anglaise – même si elle imite parfaitement les cuisines d'antan et peut se vanter de posséder une cheminée vieille de plusieurs siècles – ne serait pas complète sans une cuisinière Aga!*

ABOVE: *To decorate one of the bedrooms under the eaves, Filippa Naess called in the Argentinean painter Riccardo Cinalli who decorated the walls with half-moons and stars.*

RIGHT: *A large painting by the Belgian artist Pierre Alechinsky found a place – rather surprisingly – in the bathroom.*

FACING PAGE: *For the main drawing room, Naess chose sumptuous fabrics and carpets, taking care to cover the Georgian wing-backed armchair with its original – and very splendid – crimson velvet.*

OBEN: *Bei der Gestaltung eines der Dachzimmer wurde der argentinische Maler Riccardo Cinalli hinzugezogen, der die Wände mit Halbmonden und Sternen verzierte.*

RECHTS: *Das Gemälde des belgischen Künstlers Pierre Alechinsky hat einen originellen Platz gefunden: das Badezimmer!*

RECHTE SEITE: *Für das große Wohnzimmer hat Naess prächtige Teppiche und Stoffe ausgesucht. Der georgianische Ohrensessel hat seinen karmesinroten Originalbezug behalten.*

CI-DESSUS: *Pour décorer une des chambres sous les combles, Filippa Naess s'est assuré la collaboration du peintre argentin Riccardo Cinalli, qui a décoré les parois avec des demi-lunes et des étoiles.*

A DROITE: *Un tableau de l'artiste belge Pierre Alechinsky a trouvé une place – surprenante – dans la salle de bains!*

PAGE DE DROITE: *Pour le grand salon, Filippa a choisi des tissus et des tapis somptueux. Le fauteuil à oreilles georgien a gardé son splendide revêtement d'origine en velours cramoisi.*

KEEPER'S LODGE
Antony Little
Wiltshire

Keeper's Lodge, a 19th-century gamekeeper's cottage, properly belongs in a fairy tale by the Brothers Grimm. It nestles at the bottom of a valley in a part of Wiltshire so densely wooded that no great effort of the imagination is needed to people the glades around with gnomes, witches and such. Antony Little, whose fabric designs for Osborne and Little have made him world famous, fell in love with the abandoned Keeper's Lodge many years ago. Antony is a man who wears his love of nature very much on his sleeve, and the lush beauty of the Lodge's surroundings suited him perfectly; he therefore decided it was high time somebody shouldered the responsibility of preserving this romantic cottage in its idyllic woodland setting. Since then, he has stamped his own seal on the cluster of dingy, low-ceilinged rooms that originally made up the Lodge's interior. Drawing on his own joyous collection of flowered fabrics and wallpapers, he has created a warm, welcoming abode for himself, where he can sit by his fire with a rug across his knees, a cup of tea in one hand and a book in the other, and survey the woods beyond his leaded glass windows. The place is so perfect it is no wonder he is reluctant to share any part of it with the rest of the world.

ABOVE: *Antony Little, with a pile of fabrics designed by himself.*
LEFT: *in a guest room, a richly-coloured Indian robe.*

OBEN: *Antony Little hinter einem Stapel Stoffe aus seiner Kollektion.*
LINKS: *In einem der Gästezimmer hat Antony einen farbenfrohen indischen Mantel aufgehängt.*

CI-DESSUS: *Antony Little, posant derrière une pile de tissus créés par lui.*
A GAUCHE: *Dans une chambre d'amis, Antony a accroché un manteau indien aux couleurs somptueuses.*

Keeper's Lodge is like
the witch's house in the
story of Hansel and
Gretel.

Keeper's Lodge wäre der
ideale Ort für Hänsel
und Gretel.

Keeper's Lodge aurait
pu servir de décor à
l'histoire de Hansl et
Gretl.

Das alte Försterhaus Keeper's Lodge könnte ohne weiteres
einem Märchen der Gebrüder Grimm entsprungen sein, zumal
es sich in einem kleinen Tal in einem besonders dicht bewalde-
ten Teil von Wiltshire versteckt. Das Haus aus dem 19. Jahrhundert dürfte besonders all jenen gefallen, die noch an Zwer-
ge, Hexen und Geister glauben können. Antony Little, die eine
Hälfte des Gespanns »Osborne and Little«, das weltbekannte
Stoffe herstellt, verliebte sich vor langer Zeit in das winzige her-
untergekommene Haus. Als ein großer Naturliebhaber verfiel
er auf der Stelle der grünen Schönheit dieses Ortes, und für ihn
stand fest, daß es höchste Zeit war, das verwunschene Häus-
chen zu retten. Von Anfang an war Antony entschlossen, den
niedrigen Räumen seine ganz persönliche Note zu geben. Im
Handumdrehen verwandelte er das Labyrinth aus düsteren,
kleinen Kammern durch freundliche blumige Stoffe und Tapeten aus seiner Kollektion in eine Reihe einladender Zimmer.
Hier nimmt er gerne neben dem Kamin den Tee ein, mit einer
Decke auf dem Schoß und einem guten Buch auf den Knien,
während der Blick aus dem Fenster über den nahen Wald
schweift. Ein gut verborgenes Hexenhäuschen, das Antony auf
keinen Fall mit dem Rest der Welt teilen möchte!

Keeper's Lodge pourrait figurer dans un des contes des frères
Grimm, car cette ancienne demeure de garde-chasse du 19e
dissimulée au fond d'un vallon dans une région densément
boisée du Wiltshire, a tout pour plaire à ceux qui croient aux
histoires peuplées de gnomes, de sorcières et autres créatures
fantastiques. Antony Little, créateur de tissus à la renommée
mondiale – et la moitié du célèbre tandem «Osborne and
Little» – est tombé amoureux de ce «lodge» minuscule, aban-
donné il y a bien longtemps. Et comme il porte son amour
pour la nature en bandoulière, il a «craqué» pour la beauté verte du domaine et décidé qu'il était bien temps que quelqu'un
s'occupe de sauver cet endroit et cette maisonnette romantique
à souhait! Dès le début, il était évident qu'Antony allait mar-
quer de sa «griffe» cet ensemble de petites pièces basses et, en
un tour de main, l'apport de sa collection de tissus et de
papiers peints grouillant de dessins gais et fleuris a transformé
ce labyrinthe de cagibis sombres en une série de pièces
accueillantes où il fait bon prendre le thé à côté d'un feu de
bois, avec un plaid et un bon livre sur les genoux, tandis que
l'on regarde par les fenêtres à vitraux un paysage de carte posta-
le. Un gîte de rêve bien caché que le propriétaire heureux n'a
vraiment pas envie de partager avec le reste du monde!

The bedhead, designed
by Antony, resembles the
silhouette of a a mosque.
The fabrics and wall-
papers are from Osborne
and Little.

Das Kopfteil des Bettes
ist ein Entwurf von
Antony und erinnert an
die Silhouette einer
Moschee. Stoffe und
Tapeten stammen von
Osborne and Little.

Le dossier du lit – dessiné par Antony – évoque
la silhouette d'une mos-
quée. Les tissus et les
papiers peints sont de
Osborne and Little.

FACING PAGE: *The entrance to Keeper's Lodge is an amazing accumulation of decorative objects, laden coat rack, rubber boots, and garden tools.*
ABOVE: *The "Grand Salon" is a blend of Victorian and Edwardian taste. The pictures, the check curtains, the imitation bamboo seat and the sofa reflect a typically English delight in sentimental clutter.*
RIGHT: *Teatime… Antony Little and his wife like to take their tea as close to the fireside as possible, under a baroque carved mirror.*

LINKE SEITE: *An der Garderobe hängen zahlreiche Kleidungsstücke, und die Gummistiefel und Gartengeräte sind stets griffbereit…*
OBEN: *Der kleine »Große Salon« orientiert sich am Geschmack der viktorianischen und edwardianischen Zeit zu Beginn des 20. Jahrhunderts und belegt die typisch englische Vorliebe für romantischen Trödel.*
RECHTS: *Teatime… Antony Little und seine Frau nehmen den Tee gerne ganz nah am Kamin ein, unter einem geschnitzten Barockspiegel.*

PAGE DE GAUCHE: *Le porte-manteaux croule sous les vêtements, et les «wellies» et les outils de jardinage sont à portée de la main…*
CI-DESSUS: *Le petit «Grand Salon» s'inspire à la fois du goût de la reine Victoria et de celui qui fut en vogue sous le règne de son fils Edouard VII. Il reflète le goût typiquement anglais pour le bric-à-brac sentimental.*
A DROITE: *L'heure du thé… Antony Little et son épouse la préfèrent le plus près possible de la cheminée sous un miroir baroque en bois sculpté.*

FACING PAGE: Antony Little's favourite corner of the house. The imitation bamboo seat and the padded armchair are covered in fabrics from his collection; the landscapes and binoculars hanging on the wall hint that he still dreams of travelling to distant lands.

LEFT: Red predominates in the study of the mistress of the house. The wrought-iron daybed is covered in a fabric with an oriental pattern.

LINKE SEITE: die Lieblingsecke des Hausherrn. Der Sessel aus falschem Bambus und der Polstersessel sind mit Stoffen aus der eigenen Kollektion bezogen. Die Landschaftsgemälde an den Wänden und das Fernglas lassen keinen Zweifel daran, daß Mr. Little von fernen Ländern träumt.

LINKS: Im Arbeitszimmer der Hausherrin dominiert die Farbe Rot. Auf der schmiedeeisernen Liege ist eine Decke mit orientalischen Motiven ausgebreitet.

PAGE DE GAUCHE: le coin préféré du maître de maison. Le siège en faux bambou et le fauteuil capitonné sont recouverts d'étoffes de sa collection; quant aux paysages accrochés au mur (plus la présence de jumelles), ils nous prouvent que Mr. Little ne cesse de rêver de contrées lointaines.

A GAUCHE: Dans le bureau de la maîtresse de maison, le rouge domine. Le lit de repos en fer forgé a été recouvert d'un tissu à motif oriental.

RECHTS: Hauptthema im Eßzimmer ist die Natur – schließlich ist Antony Little ein großer Naturliebhaber und setzt sich für die Erhaltung der waldreichen Umgebung ein. Die Tapete zeigt verschiedene Motive von Buchsbaum in Tierform. Der Metalllüster im Regency-Stil hat die Form einer Ananas, zur Zeit von George IV. ein Symbol für Wohlstand.

RIGHT: The theme of the décor in the dining room is nature itself. Antony Little is passionate about this and has fought hard to preserve the marvellous setting of Keeper's Lodge. The wallpaper is patterned with box trees shaped to resemble animals and the Regency-style tin chandelier is in the form of a pineapple, a great symbol of prosperity in the reign of George IV.

A DROITE: Le thème principal de la décoration de la salle à manger est inspiré de la nature – une des grandes passions d'Antony Little qui se bat pour préserver le site merveilleux où est niché Keeper's Lodge. Le papier peint montre des buis taillés en forme d'animaux, et le lustre en tôle de style Regency a pris la forme d'un ananas, symbole de prospérité sous le règne de George IV.

LEFT: *In the down-stairs lavatory, the tiles are unexpectedly deco-rated with game and poultry. The fittings are Edwardian in style.*
FACING PAGE: *In the bathroom, a striped wallpaper makes a dis-creet background for a set of flower paintings. The claw-footed tub is made of enamelled cast iron and the fittings date from the early 20th century.*

LINKS: *Auf den Kacheln des Waschrau-mes im Erdgeschoß fin-den sich ungewöhnliche Dekorationsmotive: Geflügel und Wild. Die sanitären Anlagen ori-entieren sich am Stil der edwardianischen Zeit.*
RECHTE SEITE: *Im Badezimmer bildet das Streifenmuster einen zurückhaltenden Hin-tergrund für die Serie von Blumenbildern. Die emaillierte Bade-wanne ruht auf Klau-enfüßen. Die sanitären Anlagen stammen vom Anfang des 20. Jahr-hunderts.*

A GAUCHE: *Dans les toilettes du rez-de-chaussée, les carreaux ornés de volaille et de gibier forment un décor inattendu. Les sani-taires sont inspirés de l'époque édouardienne.*
PAGE DE DROITE: *Dans la salle de bains, un décor à rayures sert d'arrière-plan discret à une série de peintures florales. La baignoire à pieds griffus est en fonte émaillée, et les installa-tions sanitaires datent du début du 20e siècle.*

CHARLTON HOUSE
Roger and Monty Saul

Somerset

Roger Saul and the Mulberry Company are famous for Saul's unique way of communicating his passion for the beauty of leather, warm tones and opulent fabrics. For some time Saul has been wearing the mantle of ambassador for the English country look – a relaxed way of living in which nothing seems studied and in which the term "cosy" implies scuffed leather armchairs, a cup of fragrant tea and a blazing wood fire. What he lacked was a very special house in which he could bring together all these elements and more. Roger and his wife Monty were already living in a beautiful place in Somerset, but they pricked up their ears when they heard that Charlton House was on the market. Roger had visited Charlton as a child – grand hall, magnificent staircase, enormous reception rooms – and suddenly it struck him that this rambling Victorian pile was exactly the décor he craved. It is now only three years since the last workman packed his tools and left, and Charlton is already established as a luxury country hotel receiving guests from all over the world. With its stout four-poster beds, excellent restaurant, fine furniture and Mulberry fabrics and accessories, Charlton can already be counted a resounding success for Roger and Monty Saul.

In one of the drawing-room armchairs, an embroidered velvet cushion with a coat of arms, by Mulberry.

Auf einem der Sessel im Salon liegt ein besticktes, mit einem Wappen verziertes Mulberry-Samtkissen.

Sur un fauteuil du salon, on découvre un coussin en velours brodé, embelli d'un écusson, signé Mulberry.

Roger Saul und seine Mulberry Company sind berühmt für ihr Talent im Umgang mit Leder, warmen Farbtönen und opulenten Stoffen. Da Roger Saul sich seiner schwierigen Rolle als eines »Botschafters des englischen Country-Look« bewußt ist – Synonym für einen entspannten Wohnstil, in dem nichts aufgesetzt wirkt –, hat er sich auf einem ungewöhnlichen Anwesen niedergelassen, das sich ideal für seine bevorzugte Lebensweise eignet. Für ihn ist »cosyness« gleichbedeutend mit einer Tasse duftendem Tee und einem alten abgenutzten Ledersessel vor dem Kamin. Roger und seine Frau Monty bewohnten ein prächtiges Haus in Somerset und spitzten die Ohren, als sie erfuhren, daß Charlton House zum Verkauf stand! »Mister Mulberry« erinnerte sich, daß er schon einmal als Junge in das viktorianische Anwesen mit den unzähligen weitläufigen Salons eingeladen war und damals in kurzen Hosen in der großen Eingangshalle mit dem prachtvollen Treppenhaus gestanden hatte. Und er begriff mit einem Mal, daß er sein Traumhaus gefunden hatte… Drei Jahre nach Abschluß der Renovierungsarbeiten ist Charlton House ein »Country Hotel« der Luxusklasse. Gemütliche Himmelbetten, ein exzellentes Restaurant, edles Mobiliar sowie Stoffe und Accessoires von Mulberry verwandelten das alte Gebäude in ein traumhaftes Hotel.

A window embrasure transformed into a place to relax – by the simple addition of a curtain and a few richly-covered cushions.

Die Fensternische wurde durch einen Vorhang und prächtig bezogene Kissen in eine einladende Sitzecke verwandelt.

L'embrasure d'une fenêtre a été transformée en coin repos par le simple ajout d'un rideau et de coussins recouverts de tissus somptueux.

Ce qui a rendu célèbre Roger Saul et sa Mulberry Company, c'est la manière unique dont le créateur a réussi à communiquer sa passion pour la beauté du cuir, les tonalités chaudes et les tissus opulents. Et comme il est conscient de son rôle difficile d'«ambassadeur du country-look anglais» – une façon de vivre décontractée où rien ne semble étudié et où le terme «cosyness» est synonyme d'un vieux fauteuil en cuir fatigué, d'une tasse de thé parfumé et d'un bon feu de bois –, il s'est emparé d'une demeure exceptionnelle où il a réuni tous les éléments de son mode de vie préféré. Roger et son épouse Monty habitent une maison somptueuse dans le Somerset, et quand ils ont appris que Charlton House était à vendre, ils ont dressé l'oreille! «Monsieur Mulberry» se souvenait avoir été invité, tout jeune et en culottes courtes, dans cette demeure victorienne avec son grand hall et sa cage d'escalier imposante, entourée d'un grand nombre de vastes pièces de réception, et soudain il réalisa qu'il venait de trouver le décor rêvé… Trois ans après les travaux, Charlton House, devenue un «country hotel» de luxe, accueille les visiteurs venus du monde entier. Des lits à baldaquin douillets, un restaurant raffiné et des meubles, des tissus et des accessoires Mulberry font de la vieille demeure un endroit de rêve. Et Roger et Monty peuvent ajouter un succès de plus à leur palmarès éclatant.

In a corridor on the ground floor, a very beautiful Oriental carpet, fine chairs, a baroque looking glass and voluminous hangings.

Der Flur im Erdgeschoß mit einem Orientteppich, antiken Stühlen, einem barocken Spiegel und großzügig drapierten Stoffen.

Dans un couloir du rez-de-chaussée, un très beau tapis d'Orient, des sièges de style, un miroir baroque et des rideaux généreusement drapés.

In the huge living room, a multitude of arm-chairs and sofas uphol-stered with Mulberry fabrics – the very place to settle down with a tumbler of whisky and a good book.

Im geräumigen Salon laden eine Vielzahl von Sesseln und Sofas mit Mulberry-Bezügen zum Verweilen ein – der ideale Platz für lange Abende vor dem Kamin mit einem Glas Whisky!

Dans le vaste living-room, une multitude de fauteuils et de canapés recouverts de tissus Mul-berry invitent à la dou-ceur de vivre et aux longues soirées au coin du feu, un bon verre de whisky à la main!

ABOVE: *In one of the main bedrooms, the Sauls have installed an impressive Jacobean four-poster. The distinctive Mulberry style is reflected in the choice of fabrics and the velvet cushions with richly-embroidered coats of arms. The cane-backed chair is in the style of Louis Quinze.*

OBEN: *In einem der geräumigen Schlafzimmer haben die Sauls ein imposantes Himmelbett im »Jacobean-Style« aufgestellt. Den »Mulberry-Stil« erkennt man*

an reichen Stoffen und reich mit Wappen verzierten Samtkissen. Der Sessel mit Peddigrohrgeflecht ist im Louis-Quinze-Stil gehalten.

CI-DESSUS: *Dans une des chambres à coucher principales, les Saul ont installé un impressionnant lit à baldaquin jacobéen. Le «style Mulberry» se reflète dans le choix des tissus et dans la présence de coussins en velours ornés d'écussons richement brodés. Le siège canné est de style Louis Quinze.*

FACING PAGE: *In one of the first-floor bedrooms, 16th-century dark oak panelling supplies a perfect backdrop for a large double bed with a bedhead decorated with "plis serviettes" panels, a coverlet of embossed velvet embroidered with plant motifs, and abundant soft cushions.*

RECHTE SEITE: *In einem der oberen Zimmer bildet die dunkle Eichentäfelung aus dem 16. Jahrhundert den idealen Hintergrund für ein großes Bett, in dessen Kopfteil Paneele mit kunstvollen Faltwerk-*

schnitzereien eingearbeitet sind. Darauf liegen mehrere Kissen und eine Tagesdecke aus Panné-Samt, die mit Pflanzenmotiven bestickt ist.

PAGE DE DROITE: *Dans une des chambres de l'étage noble, des lambris du 16e siècle en chêne sombre forment le décor idéal pour un grand lit dont le dossier a été décoré avec des panneaux «à plis serviettes». Il est garni d'un couvre-lit en velours frappé brodé de motifs végétaux et d'un amoncellement de coussins douillets.*

THE CROOKED HOUSE
Tia and Mark Swan
Welsh Borders

The home of Tia and Mark Swan stands on top of a high green hill. From this eyrie, there is a stunning view of the wonderful rolling landscapes of the Welsh Borders. The Crooked House is quite a sight, with its collapsing roof, twisted facade and dangerously ramshackle windows, but all this is pure illusion. This totally habitable ruin, which one can only get to by way of winding muddy tracks and paths, has been saved from destruction by a couple who are passionate about old houses and who breathed new life into it by restoring it very carefully in order to preserve its dilapidated character. Mark is a restorer of old buildings and a great expert; his wife is a former teacher. Together they spent many days and nights fighting to save this farmhouse, whose origins date back to the Middle Ages. Today, the inmates of The Crooked House live happily with their old furniture and sleep under multicoloured quilts in good country beds. The old fireplaces are again in use, and the larder is full of fresh fruit, vegetables and bottles of Tia's homemade wine.

ABOVE: *The Swans sit in the sunshine on a little bench with its back to the "old" barn.*
LEFT: *Mark Swan has deliberately preserved the sagging, tumble-down character of his cottage.*

OBEN: *Die Swans genießen die Sonne auf der kleinen Bank an der »alten« Scheune.*
LINKS: *Mark Swan hat bewußt das verwitterte und baufällige Aussehen des Cottage erhalten.*

CI-DESSUS: *Les Swan profitent du soleil sur le petit banc adossé contre la «vieille» grange.*
A GAUCHE: *Mark Swan a volontairement préservé l'aspect vétuste et affaissé de son cottage.*

Das Haus von Tia und Mark Swan krönt den Gipfel eines grünen Hügels. Von ihrem »Adlerhorst« aus haben sie einen atemberaubenden Blick auf die sanft gewellte Landschaft der Welsh Borders. Mit seinem schrägen Dach, der krummen Fassade und den gefährlich geneigten Fenstern wirkt The Crooked House, das »schiefe Haus«, fast baufällig. Doch das scheint nur so, denn in der »Ruine«, die nur über verschlungene Wege und schlammige Pfade zu erreichen ist, wohnt ein Paar, das sich leidenschaftlich für »alte Steine« begeistert. Die beiden haben das Haus vor dem völligen Verfall bewahrt, ihm mit einer behutsamen Restaurierung seine Seele zurückgegeben und dabei die romantische Aura des »hohen Alters« erhalten! Lange Jahre haben Mark, der beruflich alte Häuser restauriert, und seine Frau, eine ehemalige Lehrerin, jede freie Minute daran gearbeitet, den ehemaligen Bauernhof zu retten, dessen Ursprünge bis ins Mittelalter zurückgehen. Heute liegen wieder farbenfrohe Patchwork-Quilts auf den Betten, in den alten Kaminen prasseln die Holzscheite, und die Speisekammer ist prall gefüllt mit eigenem Obst und Gemüse sowie Tias selbst hergestelltem Wein. Hier, inmitten der alten Bauernmöbel, läßt es sich gut arbeiten… oder auch in den Tag hinein leben.

From the Swans' eyrie at the top of a hill, there is a magnificent view of the Welsh border country.

Von ihrem »Adlerhorst« hoch oben auf dem grünen Hügel haben die Swans einen herrlichen Blick auf die Umgebung der Welsh Borders.

Depuis le «nid d'aigle» des Swan, situé au sommet d'une haute colline, on a une vue époustouflante sur le paysage environnant des Welsh Borders.

La maison de Tia et Mark Swan couronne une haute colline verte, et de ce nid d'aigle exceptionnel ils ont une vue époustouflante sur le magnifique paysage ondoyant des Welsh Borders. The Crooked House, «la maison biscornue», nous offre le spectacle unique de ses toits écroulés, de sa façade de guingois et de ses fenêtres dangereusement effondrées, mais tout n'est qu'illusion car cette fausse ruine habitable uniquement accessible si l'on emprunte des chemins tortueux et des sentiers boueux, a été sauvée de la destruction totale par ce couple passionné de vieilles pierres. Il lui a rendu son âme en la restaurant par touches délicates afin de préserver son allure romantique de grande invalide! Pendant de nombreuses années, Mark, restaurateur de bâtiments anciens et spécialiste hors pair, et son épouse, ex-institutrice, ont travaillé jour et nuit pour sauver cette ferme dont les origines remontent au Moyen Age. Aujourd'hui, un feu de bois crépite à nouveau dans les vieilles cheminées, le garde-manger regorge de fruits, de légumes et de vins maison, concoctés par Tia. Il fait bon vivre parmi le mobilier campagnard ancien et se reposer dans les lits rustiques couverts de «quilts» multicolores…

Mark and Tia decided that the facade of the 16th-century main house should be geranium red.

Mark und Tia haben für die Fassade des Haupthauses aus dem 16. Jahrhundert einen geranienroten Anstrich gewählt.

Mark et Tia ont décidé que la façade de la maison principale, qui date du 16ᵉ siècle, serait rouge géranium.

FACING PAGE: *In a corner of the living room, Mark has installed an old-style kitchen with a heavy stone sink.*

ABOVE: *The bench was bought from a local dealer, and the tables, chairs and kitchen utensils come from assorted junkshops. The cast-iron Victorian stove was a gift from a generous friend.*

RIGHT: *The boarding at the rear did not exist before the Swans' arrival, and the doors and cupboards were put in by Mark himself.*

LINKE SEITE: *In einer Ecke des Wohnzimmers hat Mark eine »alte« Kochstelle eingerichtet, deren Prunkstück eine solide Steinspüle ist.*

OBEN: *Die Bank stammt von einem örtlichen Antiquitätenhändler, die Tische, Stühle und Küchengeräte von verschiedenen Trödelmärkten, und der viktorianische gußeiserne Herd ist das Geschenk eines Freundes.*

RECHTS: *Die hinteren Wände wurden nachträglich eingezogen, und auch die Schränke und Türen stammen von Mark.*

PAGE DE GAUCHE: *Dans un coin du séjour, Mark a installé une cuisine à l'ancienne qui s'enorgueillit d'un robuste évier en pierre.*

CI-DESSUS: *La banquette a été achetée chez un antiquaire de la région, les tables, les chaises et les ustensiles de cuisine proviennent des brocanteurs les plus divers et la cuisinière en fonte victorienne est un cadeau d'un ami généreux.*

A DROITE: *Les parois du fond ont été posées ultérieurement et Mark a ajouté les portes et les placards.*

LEFT: *In old country houses, life invariably centres on the hearth with its log fire: the Swans' cottage is no exception. The two velvet-upholstered armchairs are Victorian, and the stone floor dates from the time when the house was built.*
FACING PAGE: *The dining room still has its original beams and whitewashed walls. The rustic furniture is mostly 18th century.*

LINKS: *In alten Landhäusern ist der Ofen mit dem knisternden Feuer das Herz des Hauses – so ist es auch bei den Swans! Die beiden viktorianischen Sessel sind mit Samt bezogen, der Steinfußboden stammt aus der Entstehungszeit des Hauses.*
RECHTE SEITE: *Das Eßzimmer verfügt noch über die originalen Deckenbalken und weiß gekalkten Wände. Die rustikalen Möbel stammen aus dem 18. Jahrhundert.*

A GAUCHE: *Dans les vieilles demeures campagnardes, la vie se joue autour de l'âtre et son feu crépitant, et celle des Swan ne fait pas exception à la règle. Les deux fauteuils recouverts de velours sont victoriens et le sol en pierre date de l'époque de la construction.*
PAGE DE DROITE: *La salle à manger a gardé ses poutres anciennes et ses murs blanchis à la chaux. Le mobilier rustique date en grande partie du 18ᵉ siècle.*

Mark built a dream larder in which Tia keeps all the products of her domestic labour: homemade wines, fruit, vegetables, cheeses and above all her delicious cakes and pies.

Mark baute diese wunderbare »Vorratskammer«, in der Tia selbst hergestellten Wein und Käse sowie eigenes Obst und Gemüse aufbewahrt – und natürlich ihre köstlichen Kuchen und »Pies«, die sie nach altem Rezept backt.

Mark a construit un «garde-manger» de rêve, et pour lui faire honneur Tia y garde pieusement le fruit de ses labeurs domestiques: vins, fruits, légumes et fromages et, surtout, ses délicieux gâteaux et «pies» à l'ancienne.

The Pink Room owes its name to the colour of its walls. The secret of this faded hue lies in the mixing of limewash with pink pigments. Mark did the painting and installed the cast-iron cooker himself. The leaded windows were put in by Tia: the result is a room of bewitching charm.

Der Rosa Salon verdankt seinen Namen dem außergewöhnlichen Farbton der Wände, den Mark nach eigenem Rezept aus Kalk und rosa Farbpigmenten herstellt. Mark baute auch den gußeisernen Herd ein, und Tia besorgte die bleiverglasten Fenster für den zauberhaften Raum.

Le Salon Rose doit son nom à la couleur rose délavée de ses murs. Son secret? Mark a mélangé de la chaux à des pigments roses. C'est lui encore qui a installé la cuisinière en fonte; Tia, elle, s'est chargée des fenêtres à vitraux. Le résultat de tous ces efforts est une pièce au charme envoûtant.

FACING PAGE: *The old pine sideboard is Tia's exclusive domain; she uses it to display her Spode and Staffordshire china.*
ABOVE: *In the dining room, the blue cupboard with its wire screen panels is actually a 19th-century meat-safe used to keep flies away from food.*
RIGHT: *The second kitchen, which Tia gaily calls her 20th-century one, still bears very little resemblance to the anti-septic, polished steel, machine-filled room to which most of us are accustomed.*

LINKE SEITE: *In der antiken Kiefernanrichte stellt Tia ihre »Schätze« aus: Steingut aus englischen Manufakturen wie Spode und Staffordshire.*
OBEN: *Der blaue Schrank im Eßzimmer, dessen Türen mit Flie-gengitter bespannt sind, stammt aus dem 19. Jahrhundert und diente ursprünglich als Speiseschrank.*
RECHTS: *Die zweite Küche nennt Tia fröhlich »ihre Küche aus dem 20. Jahrhundert«. Dennoch erinnert hier nichts an die modernen, sterilen Küchen.*

PAGE DE GAUCHE: *L'ancien buffet en pin est le domaine de Tia qui expose ici ses «trésors» en faïence provenant de manufactures anglaises renommées, telles que Spode et Staffordshire.*
CI-DESSUS: *Dans la salle à manger, l'armoire bleue équipée de panneaux en moustiquaire n'est autre qu'un garde-manger datant du 19e siècle.*
A DROITE: *Dans la seconde cuisine, celle que Tia appelle allègre-ment «ma cuisine du 20e siècle» rien n'évoque pourtant nos cuisines aseptisées.*

LEFT: *In one of the bedrooms, Tia has installed a small bathroom area, using an old washbasin, pitcher, and enamelled tin pail.*
FACING PAGE: *The privy is fairly primitive, hidden away in a wall-cupboard on the first-floor landing. According to Tia, the colour blue keeps flies away; the collection of toothbrushes was assembled partly through the forgetfulness of guests and partly through the generosity of donors.*

LINKS: *Mit einer alten Waschgarnitur und einem dazugehörigen, emaillierten Eimer hat Tia eine kleine Ecke in einem der Schlafzimmer zum »Badezimmer« umfunktioniert.*
RECHTE SEITE: *Das stille Örtchen versteckt sich hinter einem Wandschrank auf dem Treppenabsatz der ersten Etage. Laut Tia hält das Blau die Fliegen ab. Zu der Zahnbürsten-Sammlung haben vergeßliche Gäste und großzügige Spender ihren Teil beigetragen.*

A GAUCHE: *Dans une des chambres à coucher, Tia a installé un coin pour la toilette: un ancien lavabo avec un broc et son seau en métal émaillé.*
PAGE DE DROITE: *Le «Privy», des toilettes restées en l'état et dissimulées dans un placard sur le palier du premier étage. Le bleu, raconte Tia, a le pouvoir de chasser les mouches, et la collection de brosses à dents a été réalisée en grande partie grâce à des hôtes oublieux et à la générosité de quelques donateurs.*

"Entering the gate and passing the shrubs, the silhouette of a house rose to view; in seeking the door, I turned an angle: there shot out the friendly gleam again, from the lozenged panes of a very small latticed window... I could see clearly a room with a sanded floor, clean scoured; a dresser of walnut, with pewter plates ranged in rows, reflecting the redness and radiance of a glowing peat fire. I could see a clock, a white deal table, some chairs. The candle, whose ray had been my beacon, burnt on the table..."

»Sowie ich durch das Tor getreten und an den Büschen vorbeigegangen war, wurden die dunklen Umrisse eines niedrigen, länglichen Hauses sichtbar... Auf der Suche nach einer Tür bog ich um eine Ecke und da war mit einem Mal der freundliche Lichtschein wieder. Er fiel aus den rautenförmigen Scheiben eines winzigen Gitterfensters... Ich blickte in ein Zimmer mit einem blankgefegten Sandfußboden und einer Anrichte aus Walnußholz, auf der Zinnteller in Reihen angeordnet waren. In diesen spiegelte sich der rote Schein eines hellglühenden Torffeuers. Außerdem sah ich eine Uhr, einen Tisch aus Kiefernholz und einige Stühle. Die Kerze, die mir Leuchtfeuer gewesen war, brannte auf dem Tisch...«

«Après avoir franchi la barrière et dépassé les arbustes, la silhouette d'une maison se dressa devant moi... En cherchant la porte, je contournai un angle: la lueur amie reparut à travers les vitres en losange d'une minuscule fenêtre à petits carreaux... Je pus nettement distinguer une pièce au dallage soigneusement entretenu et recouvert de sable, un dressoir en noyer garni de rangées d'assiettes d'étain où se reflétait la radieuse lueur rouge d'un splendide feu de tourbe, une horloge, une table en bois blanc, quelques chaises. La chandelle, dont les rayons m'avaient servi de phare, brûlait sur la table...»

CHARLOTTE BRONTË
Jane Eyre

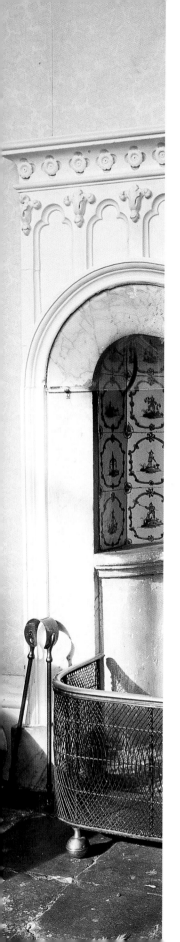

ℱRAMPTON COURT
Henrietta Clifford
Gloucestershire

On the approach to Frampton Court in the pretty village of Frampton-on-Severn, you may be caught short by the modest dimensions the house reveals when its majestic facade turns out to be no more than a brilliant trompe l'œil designed to create the illusion of enormousness. Frampton is actually a smallish 18th-century Palladian manor house, built between 1731 and 1733 by the celebrated architect John Strahan for a wealthy draper named Richard Clutterbuck. Its owner, Henrietta Clifford, who has lived here more or less forever, is perfectly satisfied with this architectural hoax. She reigns supreme in the household and attends to the wellbeing of her paying guests with a charming smile and the slightly distracted air that distinguishes the queens of enchanted places like Frampton – wearing a straw hat to go out and pick roses in her garden, and keeping a careful eye on her bedrooms with their four-poster beds and period furniture. Moreover, she is determined that her guests should fully appreciate – both at breakfast and at dinner – the fine old panelling of her dining room and the magnificent views across the park from its windows. Even better, perhaps, is the sight of Frampton's lovely neo-Gothic orangery, which stands at the end of a long pond filled with water lilies a short walk away from the main house.

ABOVE: *a view of the neo-Gothic orangery, attributed to the architect William Halfpenny.*
LEFT: *In the dining room of the orangery, the neo-Gothic fireplace is decorated with Bristol tiles imitating Delft.*

OBEN: *Blick auf die neugotische Orangerie, die der Architekt William Halfpenny entworfen hat.*
LINKS: *Der neugotische Kamin im Speisesaal der Orangerie ist mit Kacheln aus Bristol im Delfter Stil verziert.*

CI-DESSUS: *l'orangerie néogothique attribuée à l'architecte William Halfpenny.*
A GAUCHE: *Dans l'orangerie, l'âtre de la cheminée néogothique a été habillé de carrelages de Bristol, façon Delft.*

Nähert man sich Frampton Court, einem palladianischen Herrenhaus, das zwischen 1731 und 1733 im malerischen Frampton-on-Severn von dem berühmten Architekten John Strahan für den Tuchfabrikanten Richard Clutterbuck errichtet wurde, überraschen zunächst die bescheidenen Ausmaße des Gebäudes. Denn aus der Ferne läßt eine »Trompe l'œil«-Fassade Frampton Court wie einen majestätischen Palast erscheinen. Henrietta Clifford wirkt, als hätte sie schon immer hier gelebt, und ist mit ihrem architektonischen Schmuckstück sehr zufrieden. Mit charmantem Lächeln und der leicht entrückten Art einer früheren Schloßherrin regiert sie über das Anwesen und das Wohlbefinden ihrer »zahlenden Gäste«. Mit einem Strohhut auf dem Kopf schneidet sie im Garten Rosen, inspiziert die Himmelbetten und antiken Möbel in den Hotelzimmern und vergewissert sich auch, ob die Gäste – beim Frühstück ebenso wie beim Abendessen – von dem dunkel vertäfelten Speisesaal mit den hohen Fenstern einen guten Blick auf den Park haben. Die Aussicht ist in der Tat atemberaubend – besonders der Blick auf die nahegelegene neugotische Orangerie, die sich am Ende eines langen, seerosenbedeckten Kanals erhebt.

Frampton Court from the garden, with its austere Cotswold stone façade, cone-shaped yews and pretty agapanthus in pots.

Die strenge Gartenfront von Frampton Court aus Cotswold-Stein mit kegelförmig beschnittenen Eiben und hübschen Agapanthus in Tontöpfen.

Frampton Court vu côté jardin, avec sa façade sévère en pierre du Cotswold, ses ifs taillés en cône et ses jolis agapanthus en pot.

En s'approchant de Frampton Court, un manoir aux allures palladiennes, construit entre 1731 et 1733 au cœur du pittoresque village de Frampton-on-Severn par le célèbre architecte John Strahan pour Richard Clutterbuck, un richissime drapier, on est surpris par les dimensions modestes de la demeure, car en réalité les proportions palatiales de la façade majestueuse font figure de trompe-l'œil et donnent de loin l'illusion parfaite que Frampton Court est un bâtisse immense. Henrietta Clifford qui donne l'impression d'y vivre depuis toujours, se dit absolument satisfaite de cette supercherie architecturale. Elle règne sur la maison et sur le bien-être de ses hôtes payants avec un sourire charmant et l'air un peu distrait des souveraines des domaines enchantés, arborant le chapeau de paille pour aller cueillir les roses du jardin, s'occupant méticuleusement de ses chambres d'hôtes équipées de lits à baldaquin et d'un mobilier d'époque et s'affairant pour que ses invités – au déjeuner comme au dîner – apprécient pleinement sa salle à manger aux lambris sombres et jouissent au maximum de la vue splendide qu'offrent les grandes fenêtres sur son parc. Une vue à couper le souffle, car l'orangerie de style néogothique qui se trouve à deux pas du manoir, au bout d'un long canal où foisonnent les nymphéas, semble sortie tout droit d'un conte de fées!

Mrs Clifford, elegant as ever, basking in the sunshine with her faithful terrier Mole.

Die stets elegante Mrs. Clifford genießt die Sonne in Gesellschaft ihres treuen Begleiters Mole.

Mrs. Clifford, toujours élégante, profite du soleil en compagnie de Mole, son fidèle compagnon.

LEFT: *In the hall Mrs Clifford has composed an amusing still life by juxtaposing a child's bentwood chair and a fine early 18th-century Queen Anne chair. The fox's head is a doorstop.*
FACING PAGE: *The hall with its décor of Doric pilasters has always been used as a reception room. The chairs around the heavy table were made in the reign of George III (1760–1820).*

LINKS: *Im Eingangs-bereich hat Mrs. Clif-ford ein originelles Stilleben aus einem Kinderstuhl und einem sehr schönen Queen-Anne-Stuhl aus dem frühen 18. Jahrhundert arrangiert. Der Fuchs-kopf dient als Tür-stopper.*
RECHTE SEITE: *Seit jeher dient der Ein-gangsbereich mit den dorischen Pilastern als Empfangshalle. Die Stühle um den massiven Tisch stammen aus der Zeit von George III. (1760–1820).*

A GAUCHE: *Dans le hall d'entrée Mrs. Clifford a composé une nature morte amusante en juxtaposant une chaise d'enfant en bois cintré et un très beau siège cabriolet. La tête de renard est un «door-stop» (arrêt de porte).*
PAGE DE DROITE: *Le hall d'entrée, avec son décor à pilastres doriques sert depuis toujours de salle de réception. Les chaises autour de la table massive sont d'époque George III (1760–1820).*

LEFT: *In the drawing room, a comfortable sofa reaches out its arms towards the fireplace. The tea table, the cylinder desk, the rocaille mirror and the porcelain statuettes date from the 18th century. The sides of the fireplace are faced with Bristol tiles in the style of Delft.*

FACING PAGE: *In the oak-panelled dining room, the sideboard is Regency style and the family portrait of a woman dates from the early 20th century.*

LINKS: *Im Salon reckt das bequeme Sofa seine Armlehnen dem Kamin entgegen. Das Tee-Tischchen, der Rollsekretär, der mit Rocaillen verzierte Spiegel und die Porzellanfigürchen stammen aus dem 18. Jahrhundert. Die Seitenteile des Kamins sind mit Kacheln aus Bristol im Delfter Stil verkleidet.*

RECHTE SEITE: *Über der Regency-Anrichte im Speisesaal hängt das Porträt eines Familienmitglieds vom Anfang des 20. Jahrhunderts.*

A GAUCHE: *Dans le salon, un canapé confortable tend les bras vers la grande cheminée. La table à thé, le bureau cylindre, le miroir-rocaille et les statuettes en porcelaine datent du 18ᵉ siècle. Les «joues» de l'âtre sont tapissées de carreaux de Bristol, imitant le Delft.*

PAGE DE DROITE: *Dans la salle à manger lambrissée de chêne, le buffet est de style Regency et le portrait représente un membre de la famille.*

CHRISTOPHER GIBBS

Oxfordshire

The nostalgia and the tenderest memories of our childhoods often take unexpected turns and forms, and one is tempted to wonder to what point antique dealer Christopher Gibbs was influenced by a longing to resurrect the images of his youth, so eager has he been to reconstruct from memory the interiors of his family home. The house was built in the 19th century in the mock Tudor style from plans drawn up by the architect Sir George Gilbert Scott. It overlooks the Upper Thames Valley and offers a panorama as far as the eye can see over and beyond a pretty red brick bridge – built by Christopher's great grandfather – to the lovely landscapes of Oxfordshire. When Christopher inherited the place it was in a predestined state of run-down half-emptiness. But Christopher happens to possess a prodigious memory for furniture, objects and atmospheres; by putting this memory to work, he has been able to recreate the former décor of his house down to the tiniest detail. He maintains that "… home in the country is where the heart is" and doubtless this is the key to his personality. It also lies at the root of his love for this old house, with its studied rooms full of furniture, statues, mirrors, paintings, carpets and engravings from every epoch. The result is a private, intensely romantic place of light and shade, each corner offering some kind of window on the past.

ABOVE: *a smiling face drawn by a mischievous child on one of the frosted panes of the greenhouse.*
LEFT: *In the doorway, a Gothic stone angel salutes all comers.*

OBEN: *Auf die eisbedeckten Fenster eines Gewächshauses hat ein Frechdachs ein lachendes Gesicht gezeichnet!*
LINKS: *In der Säulenhalle begrüßt ein gotischer Engel aus Sandstein den Besucher.*

CI-DESSUS: *Sur un carreau givré d'une des serres, un polisson a tracé naïvement les traits d'un visage souriant!*
A GAUCHE: *Dans le portique, un ange en pierre de style gothique accueille les visiteurs.*

Nostalgie und schöne Kindheitserinnerungen bewirken oft unerwartete Wendungen in unserem Leben. Man kann dar-über spekulieren, inwiefern der Antiquitätenhändler Christopher Gibbs Bilder seiner Jugendtage auferstehen lassen wollte, als er sich daran machte, das Haus seiner Ahnen wieder so einzurichten, wie es in seiner Erinnerung lebte. Es war im 19. Jahrhundert nach einem Entwurf des Architekten Sir George Gilbert Scott in Anlehnung an den Tudor-Stil erbaut worden und überragt das obere Themsetal. Von hier aus bietet sich ein einzigartiger Panoramablick auf die schöne Landschaft von Oxfordshire und auf eine hübsche rote Ziegelsteinbrücke, die Christophers Ur-Großvater errichtet hatte. Es war wohl Bestimmung, daß ausgerechnet Christopher das halbleere her-untergekommene Haus erbte. Dank seines erstaunlichen Gedächtnisses für Möbel, Gegenstände und Atmosphäre konnte er das Interieur seiner Kindertage bis ins kleinste Detail rekonstruieren. Das Motto von Gibbs lautet: »Home in the country is where the heart is« und sagt viel über seine Persön-lichkeit und seine Liebe zu dem alten Haus. An den Wänden befinden sich Tapeten von William Morris, daneben gibt es sorgfältig ausgewählte Möbel, Statuen, Spiegel, Gemälde, Teppiche und Stiche aus verschiedenen Epochen. Im roman-tischen Halbdunkel der Räume öffnen sich dann die Türen zur Vergangenheit.

Seen from the garden, the Victorian Tudor facade looks austere and enigmatic.

Blick vom Garten auf die strenge Fassade im Tudor-Stil.

Vue du jardin, la mai-son aux allures vague-ment Tudor, nous offre sa façade austère et énigmatique.

A panoramic view from the garden terraces, with the bridge and the Thames valley beyond.

Die Gartenterrassen bieten einen herrlichen Blick auf die Brücke und das Themsetal.

Les terrasses du jardin offrent une vue panora-mique sur le pont et sur la vallée de la Tamise.

La nostalgie et les plus tendres souvenirs de notre enfance prennent souvent une tournure inattendue, et on peut se demander à quel point l'antiquaire Christopher Gibbs a été influencé par le désir de faire revivre les images de sa jeunesse, pour qu'il s'acharne à reconstruire – de mémoire – les inté-rieurs de sa maison ancestrale. Construite au 19e siècle dans un style vaguement élizabethain d'après un projet de l'architecte Sir George Gilbert Scott, surplombant le Upper Thames Valley et offrant un panorama à perte de vue sur un joli pont en brique rouge – édifié par son arrière-grand-père – sur le beau paysage de l'Oxfordshire, la demeure parvint à Christopher dans un état prédestiné, à moitié vide et défraîchie, et comme il possède une mémoire prodigieuse pour les meubles, les objets et, surtout, les ambiances, il a su recréer le décor d'antan dans les moindres détails. Citons Gibbs et son «Home in the country is where the heart is» (Là où est le cœur, c'est là qu'est la maison) et nous touchons à l'essentiel de sa personnalité, à son amour pour cette vieille maison aux pièces tapissées d'un papier peint William Morris et abritant un amoncellement – étudié – de meubles, de statues, de miroirs, de tableaux, de tapis et de gravures de toutes les époques. Rien d'étonnant donc si ces pièces, où règne un clair-obscur romanesque, se transforment en fenêtres sur le passé.

LEFT: *An ancient stone sphinx covered with moss squats in a peaceful corner of the garden.*
FACING PAGE: *Christopher Gibbs built his conservatory using salvaged materials and much older fragments. The marble sarcophagus is Roman and the lantern is Moroccan.*

LINKS: *In einer ruhigen Ecke des Gartens kauert eine alte moosbedeckte Sphinx.*
RECHTE SEITE: *Christopher Gibbs ließ den Wintergarten aus wiederverwendeten Materialien und antiken Fragmenten errichten. Der marmorne Sarkophag ist römisch, und die Laterne stammt aus Marokko.*

A GAUCHE: *Une très ancienne sphinge en pierre moussue est accroupie dans un coin paisible du jardin.*

PAGE DE DROITE: *Christopher Gibbs a fait construire le «conservatory» avec des matériaux de récupération d'époque et des fragments anciens. Le sarcophage en marbre est romaine et la lanterne est originaire du Maroc.*

RIGHT: *Few things are more restful than the tinkle of a fountain flowing into a moss-covered basin.*

RECHTS: *Es gibt nichts Entspannenderes als das Murmeln des Wassers in dem moosbewachsenen Becken eines alten Brunnens.*

A DROITE: *Rien de plus apaisant que le murmure d'une vieille fontaine qui déverse son eau dans un bassin couvert de mousse.*

LEFT: *In the hall on the garden side of the house, the shelves of a bookcase are filled with rare and precious books.*
FACING PAGE: *Near the door leading into the garden, Christopher has installed a neo-Gothic seat; on a piece of furniture made from pieces of 16th-century woodwork stands a fragment of marble representing part of the torso of a Greek "Kouros". The engraving is of the Panshanger Oak in Hertfordshire.*

LINKS: *In der Halle an der Gartenseite lädt die Bibliothek mit wertvollen und seltenen Büchern zum Stöbern ein.*
RECHTE SEITE: *Neben der Tür, die zum Garten führt, steht ein neugotischer Stuhl. Auf einem Möbelstück, das aus Holzelementen aus dem 16. Jahrhundert zusammengesetzt wurde, steht das Fragment eines griechischen »Kouros« aus Marmor. Der Stich zeigt die Eiche »Panshanger Oak« in Hertfordshire.*

A GAUCHE: *Dans le hall, côté jardin, les rayonnages d'une bibliothèque regorgent de volumes rares et précieux.*
PAGE DE DROITE: *Près de la porte qui donne sur le jardin, Christopher a placé un siège néogothique et, sur un meuble composé jadis avec des éléments de boiserie du 16ᵉ siècle, il a posé un fragment de marbre représentant une partie du torse d'un kouros grec. La gravure représente le chêne «Panshanger Oak» dans le Hertfordshire.*

"So my room is really just for me with all the secret things that speak to me of life and love and anchor me down here, family relics, things that I have always known set off by things that are perfect for their purpose. My favourite books are there for endless reordering and there are old watercolours of the church and river and fields mixed up with the family and their houses…"

»Und so ist das Zimmer wirklich nur für mich, mit all den geheimen Dingen, die mir vom Leben und der Liebe erzählen. Sie geben mir Wurzeln, diese Familienreliquien. Dinge, die ich immer schon um mich hatte, stehen hier neben Dingen, die perfekt ihren Zweck erfüllen. Hier sind auch meine Lieblingsbücher, die ich immer wieder lesen werde, und auch die alten Aquarelle von der Kirche, dem Fluß und den Feldern und dazwischen Bilder von meiner Familie und ihren Häusern…«

«Ainsi ma chambre est-elle vraiment à moi seul, avec toutes les choses secrètes qui me parlent de vie et d'amour et me retiennent ici, des reliques familiales, des choses que j'ai toujours connues et des choses parfaitement adaptées à leur fonction. Mes livres préférés sont ici pour être rangés sans fin et il y a de vieilles aquarelles représentant l'église et la rivière et les champs au-delà mélangées avec la famille et leurs maisons…»

CHRISTOPHER GIBBS
quoted from · zitiert aus · extrait de
The Englishman's Room

FACING PAGE: *The
seat in the bow window
of the dining room is covered with an antique
lemon-yellow chintz. It
forms a vivid contrast
with the green Victorian
woodwork and the rasp-
berry-coloured cushions.*
ABOVE: *In his drawing
room, Gibbs shows his
mastery of eclecticism by
uniting copies of Transi-
tion armchairs by Syrie
Maugham, an 18th-cen-
tury commode and a
Moroccan "Haïti".*
RIGHT: *a large earthen-
ware dish from Nider-
viller in Lorraine placed
on the seat of an
18th-century chair.*

LINKE SEITE: *Im Erker
des Eßzimmers steht eine
Eckbank mit einem alten
zitronengelben Chintz-
Überwurf. Der Kontrast
zu der grünen viktoriani-
schen Vertäfelung und
den himbeerfarbenen
Kissen ist verblüffend.*
OBEN: *Im Salon kombi-
niert Gibbs Kopien von
Transition-Stühlen von
Syrie Maugham, eine
Kommode aus dem
18. Jahrhundert und einen
marokkanischen »Haïti«-
Patchwork-Quilt.*
RECHTS: *Der Fayence-
Teller aus dem lothringi-
schen Niderviller steht auf
einem Armlehnstuhl aus
dem 18. Jahrhundert.*

PAGE DE GAUCHE:
*Une banquette installée
dans l'embrasure du
bow-window de la salle
à manger est garnie d'un
chintz ancien jaune. Le
contraste avec les boise-
ries vertes victoriennes et
les deux coussins fram-
boise est surprenant.*
CI-DESSUS: *Dans son
salon, Gibbs marie des
copies de fauteuils Tran-
sition signées Syrie Mau-
gham, une commode 18^e
signée Saunier et un
patchwork «Haïti»
marocain.*
A DROITE: *une grande
assiette en faïence de
Niderviller en Lorraine
posée sur une chaise 18e.*

ABOVE: The iron and brass Victorian bedstead is surrounded by "old pink" walls hung with a series of engravings by Thomas Patch (c. 1725–1782). The counterpane is in 17th-century "crewelwork".

RIGHT AND FACING PAGE: In one of the bathrooms, the gothic inspired cupboard with mirror came from Ireland. On the washstand Gibbs has placed a silver-encrusted looking glass from Ceylon. On the windowsill stands a 19th-century Turkish goblet and pitcher.

OBEN: In Altrosa gehaltene Wände umgeben das viktorianische Bettgestell aus Eisen und Messing. Die Stiche stammen von Thomas Patch (c. 1725–1782). Die Tagesdecke aus dem 17. Jahrhundert ist in der »Crewelwork«-Technik gearbeitet.

RECHTS UND RECHTE SEITE: Der gotisch anmutende Schrank in einem der Badezimmer stammt aus Irland, der Toilettenspiegel mit Silberinkrustationen aus Ceylon. Auf der Fensterbank steht ein türkisches Waschzeug aus dem 19. Jahrhundert.

CI-DESSUS: Le lit victorien en fer et laiton est entouré de murs couleur vieux rose, envahis par une série de gravures signées Thomas Patch (vers 1725–1782). Le couvre-lit du 17e siècle est en «crewelwork».

A DROITE ET PAGE DE DROITE: Dans une salle de bains, l'armoire d'inspiration gothique provient d'Irlande. Sur le meuble qui abrite le lavabo, Gibbs a posé un miroir de toilette de Ceylan aux incrustations d'argent. Sur l'appui de fenêtre on aperçoit une coupe et une cruche turques du 19e siècle.

THE MANOR HOUSE
Bettina and Lawrence Bachmann
Oxfordshire

Mrs Bettina Bachmann is the very model of chic, and the same goes for her 17th-century manor in Oxfordshire. The house is austere in aspect, built of stone, with an old garden full of clipped yew hedges; its views across the green, rolling countryside are incomparable. Mrs Bachmann does not care for the English style with its flowered chintz, voluminous curtains, and flounced slipcovers. Rather, her preference is for "windows without fringes", straightforward colours and furniture with pure, unfussy lines. You have only to cross the threshold into the vast hall of her house, where the walls are the colour of chocolate and the space is dominated by a massive head of Antinous – a late 18th-century copy in Coade Stone – to become aware of Mrs Bachmann's iconoclasm. As it turns out, Bettina and Lawrence Bachmann have always rather specialised in shocking the bourgeoisie. They are used to people letting out cries of amazement at the sight of their sparsely-furnished, "cauliflower-coloured" dining room with its bulky table, wrought-iron chandelier and slipcovered folding chairs. Ditto the library, where most of the books and shelves are trompe l'œil, and even the bedroom, which is Edinburgh Rock Pink, with an enormous latticework bedstead painted orange.

ABOVE: *the elegant Georgian-style kitchen window.*
LEFT: *In the front hall stands the head of the handsome Antinous – an 18th-century copy in Coade Stone after the original in the Louvre.*

OBEN: *das elegante georgianische Küchenfenster.*
LINKS: *Die Antinoos-Büste in der Eingangshalle ist eine aus »Coade Stone« gefertigte Kopie aus dem 18. Jahrhundert nach dem Original im Louvre.*

CI-DESSUS: *dans la cuisine, une élégante fenêtre de style georgien.*
A GAUCHE: *Dans le hall d'entrée, une tête représentant le bel Antinoüs – une copie du 18ᵉ en «Coade stone» d'après l'original du Louvre.*

Madame Bettina Bachmann und ihr Herrenhaus aus dem 17. Jahrhundert in Oxfordshire sind die Inkarnation von Schick und Eleganz. Das strenge Steingebäude umgibt ein alter Garten mit beschnittenen Eibenhecken, der eine herrliche Sicht auf die sanft gewellte grüne Landschaft gewährt. Madame Bachmann macht sich nichts aus dem englischen Stil mit seinen geblümten Chintz-Stoffen und den zahlreichen Vorhängen und Rüschenbezügen. Sie zieht »Fenster ohne Fransen« vor und schätzt Möbel mit klaren Formen und Farben. Wenn man die große Eingangshalle mit den schokoladenbraunen Wänden und der riesigen Antinoos-Büste betritt – einer Kopie der Coade Artificial Stone Manufactory aus dem späten 18. Jahrhundert –, erkennt man sofort, daß man es hier mit einer »Bilderstürmerin« zu tun hat. Übrigens sind Bettina und Lawrence Bachmann darauf spezialisiert, die Bourgeoisie zu erschrecken. Sie lieben die überraschten Ausrufe ihrer Gäste beim Anblick des blumenkohlfarbenen Eßzimmers, das mit einem großen Tisch, einem schmiedeeisernen Kronleuchter und bezogenen Klappstühlen vergleichsweise spartanisch eingerichtet ist. Unkonventionell sind auch die Bibliothek mit gemalten Büchern und Regalen und das Schlafzimmer im Farbton »Edinburgh Rock Pink«, dessen majestätisches Bett orange lackiert ist!

The manor dates from the 17th century, and the severity of its architecture provided the Bachmanns with the perfect stock on which to graft their own resolutely contemporary décor.

Das Herrenhaus aus dem 17. Jahrhundert mit seiner strengen Architektur bildet das ideale Ambiente für den konsequent modernen Einrichtungsstil der Bachmanns.

Le manoir date du 17e siècle et la rigidité de son architecture offrait aux Bachmann une base idéale pour y greffer une décoration résolument contemporaine.

Chic, chic, chic, le terme sied parfaitement à la personnalité de Madame Bettina Bachmann, et il en est de même pour son manoir du 17e dans l'Oxfordshire, un bâtiment en pierre aux lignes sévères, entouré d'un vieux jardin et de haies en if taillées, qui offre une vue splendide sur le paysage verdoyant aux doux contours. Madame Bachmann n'aime pas le style anglais et ses chintz fleuris, son amoncellement de rideaux et de housses à volants et son avalanche de petits bibelots précieux. Elle préfère des fenêtres «sans franges», un mobilier aux lignes pures et des couleurs franches. Chez elle, il suffit de franchir le seuil et de traverser le grand hall avec ses murs chocolat et son immense tête d'Antinoüs – copie de la Coade Artificial Stone Manufactory de la fin du 18e siècle – pour se rendre compte de ses goûts iconoclastes. D'ailleurs Bettina et Lawrence Bachmann n'ont jamais cessé «d'étonner le bourgeois». Ils connaissent par cœur les cris de surprise que provoquent leur salle à manger couleur de chou-fleur, à peine meublée d'une grande table, d'un lustre en fer forgé et, de chaises pliantes houssées, ainsi que leur bibliothèque ornée d'un trompe-l'œil représentant des rayons de livres, et leur chambre à coucher couleur «Edinburgh Rock Pink» où trône un lit majestueux en treillage orange!

The absence of curtains and the presence of garden furniture with very pure lines serve to emphasise the austerity of the facade.

Der Verzicht auf Vorhänge und die klare Linienführung der Gartenmöbel heben die strenge Architektur der Fassade hervor.

L'absence de rideaux et la présence d'un mobilier de jardin aux lignes épurées accentuent l'austérité de la façade.

FACING PAGE: *Bettina Bachmann chose a bitter chocolate shade for the walls of the majestic front hall. The trompe l'œil ribbons are by Paula Dellow and the big table made of metal and "faux marbre" was designed by Bettina. The head of Antinous dates from the late 18th century.*
ABOVE: *The "cauliflower-coloured" dining room is very soberly furnished. The wrought-iron chandelier is by Marston & Langinger.*
RIGHT: *the "mascherone" of the fireplace in the front hall.*

LINKE SEITE: *Die Wände der imposanten Eingangshalle erhielten den Farbton »Zartbitterschokolade«. Die »Trompe l'œil«-Bänder fertigte Paula Dellow an. Der Tisch aus Metall und falschem Marmor ist ein Entwurf von Bettina. Die Antinoos-Büste stammt aus dem 18. Jahrhundert.*
OBEN: *Das blumenkohlfarbene Eßzimmer ist nur sparsam eingerichtet. Der Kronleuchter stammt von Marston & Langinger.*
RECHTS: *die Maske auf dem Kaminsims in der Eingangshalle.*

PAGE DE GAUCHE: *Bettina Bachmann a choisi un ton «chocolat noir» pour les parois du majestueux hall d'entrée. Les rubans en trompe-l'œil sont de la main de Paula Dellow et la table en métal et faux marbre est dessinée par Bettina. La tête d'Antinoüs date du 18ᵉ siècle.*
CI-DESSUS: *La salle à manger aux doux tons de «cauliflower» a été meublée sobrement. Le chandelier en fer forgé est de Marston & Langinger.*
A DROITE: *le «mascherone» de la cheminée dans le hall.*

FACING PAGE: *Bettina had some trompe l'œil panels in the library painted to represent shelves stuffed with books. The painter, Roland Gold, declined to put titles on the spines, to prevent people from getting a crick in the neck searching for books by Proust or Joyce.*

LINKE SEITE: *Auf einige Wandpaneele in der Bibliothek ließ Bettina »Trompe l'œil«-Malereien anbringen, die Bücherregale vortäuschen. Der Künstler Roland Gold weigerte sich allerdings, die Bücher mit Titeln zu versehen, »damit die Besucher sich nicht den Hals verrenken auf der Suche nach einem Roman von Proust oder Joyce«.*

PAGE DE GAUCHE: *Sur certains panneaux de la bibliothèque, Bettina a fait réaliser des trompe-l'œil représentant des rayons bourrés de livres. Le peintre Roland Gold refusa quant à lui de doter les volumes de leurs titres «pour que le visiteur curieux ne se torde pas le cou en cherchant à y trouver un roman de Proust ou de Joyce.»*

ABOVE: *In front of a wall decorated with trompe l'œil books, Bettina has placed a simple rattan couch and a low table.*

OBEN: *Vor eine Wand mit aufgemalten Büchern hat die Hausherrin eine einfache Rattanliege und ein niedriges Tischchen gestellt.*

CI-DESSUS: *Devant un mur décoré de livres en trompe-l'œil, la maîtresse de maison a placé une simple méridienne en rotin et une table basse.*

A painting of sheep by
Roland Gold dominates
the library from its place
above the monumental
18th-century mantel-
piece sculpted by
William Collins. The
rattan furniture is from
the Conran Shop.

In der Bibliothek fällt
über dem monumenta-
len Kamin von William
Collins aus dem 18.
Jahrhundert Roland
Golds Gemälde ins
Auge, das Schafe zeigt.
Die Rattanmöbel stam-
men aus dem Conran
Shop.

Un tableau signé
Roland Gold et repré-
sentant des moutons
domine la bibliothèque
du haut de la cheminée
monumentale 18e sculp-
tée par William Collins.
Le mobilier en rotin a
été déniché au Conran
Shop.

LEFT: The high-risk juxtaposition of shocking pink and orange in the bedroom is called "Edinburgh Rock" by Bettina. It was also her decision to paint the neo-Gothic chair white, and to have the gazebo-shaped latticework bed made by Andrew Brant.

LINKS: Der sehr gewagte Kontrast aus »Shocking Pink« und Orange im Schlafzimmer wurde von Bettina »Edinburgh Rock Pink« getauft. Sie entschied auch, daß der neugotische Stuhl weiß gestrichen werden sollte, und bat Andrew Brant, ein Spalierbett in Form eines Gartenpavillons zu bauen.

A GAUCHE: «Edinburgh Rock Pink», c'est le nom que Bettina a donné à la juxtaposition très risquée du «Shocking Pink» et de l'oran-

ge dans la chambre à coucher. C'est encore elle qui a décidé que la chaise néogothique devait être peinte en blanc et qui a demandé à Andrew Brant de lui construire un lit en treillis en forme de gazebo (une sorte de belvédère, de pavillon de jardin en vogue au 18e siècle).

RECHTS: Im Badezimmer finden sich die Farben Rosa und Orange. Die Badewanne wurde auf ein vom Klassizismus inspiriertes schmiedeeisernes Gestell gesetzt.

RECHTE SEITE: Bettina Bachmann hat das Badezimmer mit zahlreichen Schränkchen ausgestattet. Durch die Verwendung von Rosa und Orange ergibt sich ein sehr interessanter Schachbretteffekt.

RIGHT: In the bathroom – also pink and orange – the cast-iron tub has been mounted on a classically-inspired wrought-iron stand.

FACING PAGE: Bettina Bachmann has equipped her bathroom with plenty of closets. The alternating pink and orange hues create a lively chequerboard effect.

A DROITE: Dans la salle de bains également rose et orange, la baignoire en fonte a été montée dans une armure en fer forgé d'inspiration classique.

PAGE DE DROITE: Bettina Bachmann a équipé sa salle de bains de nombreux placards. L'alternance du rose et de l'orange crée un effet de damier amusant.

CEDAR LODGE
Patricia and Guy Croft
Oxfordshire

When they bought the former home of the celebrated novelist Iris Murdoch (1919–1999), the banker Guy Croft and his wife Patricia shouldered the somewhat onerous task of preserving its original aspect and highly personal ambiance. Patricia, who has a passion for horses and all things equestrian, also happens to be an interior decorator of distinction – so it was understandable that she wanted to set her own seal on the fine old 18th-century building with its big walled garden. Without in any way impugning the memory of Iris Murdoch, who loved Cedar Lodge and wrote some of her finest novels under its roof, Patricia set to work on the interior in her own way. In doing so, she proved that her daring palette of canary yellow, bright cornflower blue and apple green was exactly right for the faded though still charming rooms of the house. After Guy's death, Patricia left Cedar Lodge, but she remembers with a smile that her yellow and blue bedroom – "it was as pretty and gaudy as a tropical bird" – made an explosive impact on visitors. Her green bathroom and the furniture she had made to her own design were equally successful. The Crofts did not change much in the kitchen. As for the garden, they were sensitive enough to leave the old plantings, walls and stable doors well alone, creating the effect of semi-abandon so beloved by Romantic painters.

ABOVE: *Patricia Croft with one of her favourite horses.*
LEFT: *A sundial held up by a lead cherub.*

OBEN: *Patricia Croft mit einem ihrer Lieblingspferde.*
LINKS: *Ein Engel aus Blei, der eine Sonnenuhr hält, treibt seinen Schalk in einer Ecke des Gartens.*

CI-DESSUS: *Patricia Croft avec un de ses chevaux favoris.*
A GAUCHE: *Un chérubin en plomb tenant un cadran solaire égaye un coin du jardin de sa présence espiègle.*

Als der Bankier Guy Croft und seine Frau Patricia das Haus kauften, das früher einmal der berühmten Schriftstellerin Iris Murdoch (1919–1999) gehört hatte, stellten sie sich die schwierige Aufgabe, den Originalcharakter des Hauses sowie seine sehr persönliche Atmosphäre zu bewahren. Patricia ist eine begeisterte Reiterin, aber eine ebenso talentierte Innenausstatterin. Sie brannte darauf, diesem schönen Gebäude aus dem 18. Jahrhundert und seinem hinter einer Mauer versteckten Garten ihre persönliche Note zu verleihen. Voller Respekt vor Iris Murdoch – die das Haus sehr geliebt und hier einige ihrer besten Romane geschrieben hatte – nahm sie sich die Inneneinrichtung vor und bewies, daß die gewagte Farbpalette – von Kanariengelb über Kornblumenblau bis Apfelgrün – den leicht verblichenen Charme der Räume hervorragend zur Geltung bringt. Nach dem Tod von Guy trennte sich Patricia von Cedar Lodge, doch sie erinnert sich mit einem Lächeln daran, daß ihr gelb-blaues Schlafzimmer – so »kreischend wie ein exotischer Vogel« – bei neugierigen Besuchern stets wie eine Bombe eingeschlagen war. Auch das grüne Badezimmer mit den von ihr selbst entworfenen Möbeln hatte für Aufruhr gesorgt! Doch in der Küche beließen die Crofts alles, wie es war, und auch im Garten weigerten sie sich, den alten Pflanzenbeständen, Mauern oder Stalltüren zu Leibe zu rücken.

By adding an entrance in the form of a Victorian greenhouse, the Crofts succeeded in softening the austere lines of the 18th-century facade.

Die Crofts fügten einen Eingang in Form eines viktorianischen Gewächshauses hinzu, der die Strenge der Fassade aus dem 18. Jahrhundert mildert.

En ajoutant une entrée en forme de serre victorienne, les Croft ont adouci les lignes austères de la façade 18ᵉ.

En acquérant jadis la demeure d'un personnage aussi célèbre que la romancière Iris Murdoch (1919–1999), le banquier Guy Croft et son épouse Patricia devaient assumer la lourde tâche de lui garder son aspect original et son ambiance très personnelle. D'autre part, Patricia qui, en dehors de sa passion pour les plaisirs équestres, couve une égale passion pour la décoration et mérite pleinement le titre de décoratrice d'intérieur, trépignait d'envie de poser son empreinte sur cette belle bâtisse du 18ᵉ entourée d'un grand jardin muré. Et sans manquer de respect à Murdoch qui adorait cette maison et qui écrivit ici quelques-uns de ses romans les plus poignants, elle s'attaqua aux intérieurs et prouva que sa palette osée – composée de jaune canari, d'un bleu barbeau éclatant et de vert pomme – était le choix parfait pour cet ensemble de pièces au charme suranné. Après la mort de Guy, Patricia se sépara de Cedar Lodge mais elle se souvient, avec le sourire, que sa chambre à coucher jaune et bleue et «joliment criarde comme un oiseau exotique» faisait l'effet d'une bombe auprès des curieux qui venaient voir ses transformations. Et sa salle de bains verte et la série de meubles exécutée d'après ses dessins connurent le même succès au parfum de scandale! Côté cuisine, les Croft ne touchèrent à rien; côté jardin, ils firent preuve de la même sensibilité en refusant de toucher aux anciennes plantations, aux murs et aux portes vétustes des écuries, créant ainsi l'effet d'un jardin à l'abandon.

Behind the house, a cast-iron Victorian table and chairs afford a charming place to relax.

Hinter dem Haus entstand eine charmante kleine Ruheecke mit einem gußeisernen viktorianischen Tisch und einigen Stühlen.

Derrière la maison, une table et des chaises victoriennes en fonte forment un coin-repos charmant.

LEFT: *an old wooden wheelbarrow, filled with pine cones destined for the many fireplaces of Cedar Lodge.*
FACING PAGE: *The Crofts, in their eagerness to keep the house as authentic as possible, preferred not to replace this ramshackle stable door.*

LINKS: *Die alte hölzerne Schubkarre ist mit Tannenzapfen gefüllt, die bald in den zahlreichen Kaminen des Hauses knisternd brennen werden.*
RECHTE SEITE: *Die Crofts, die das Haus möglichst ursprünglich belassen wollten, haben diese verfallene Tür zu den Pferdeställen bewußt nicht erneuert.*

A GAUCHE: *une vieille brouette en bois, remplie de pommes de pin qui serviront à alimenter les nombreuses cheminées de la maison.*
PAGE DE DROITE: *Les Croft, soucieux de préserver les éléments authentiques, ont préféré ne pas remplacer cette porte délabrée qui donne accès aux écuries.*

RIGHT: *A disused garden bench, painted Mediterranean blue, adds a note of colour.*
FAR RIGHT: *Who would guess that the stables are hidden behind this wall, with its riot of climbing plants?*

RECHTS: *Eine ausrangierte, in Meerblau gestrichene Gartenbank bildet nun einen Farbtupfer.*
GANZ RECHTS: *Wer hätte erwartet, daß sich hinter diesem von Kletterpflanzen überwucherten Mauerstück die Pferdeställe befinden?*

A DROITE: *Un ancien banc de jardin désaffecté peint en bleu méditerranéen apporte une note de couleur.*
A L'EXTRÊME DROITE: *Qui devinerait que les écuries de la propriété se cachent derrière ce pan de mur envahi par des plantes grimpantes?*

LEFT: *the old kitchen, with Windsor chairs, a rustic table and bench, and a collection of old baskets hanging from linen racks overhead.*
FACING PAGE: *Patricia has the gift of transforming the most ordinary objects into a still life: here, a potted geranium and a few stones on a window sill.*

LINKS: *In der alten Küche stehen schlichte Windsor-Stühle, ein Tisch und eine rustikale Bank. Sehr pittoresk wirkt die Sammlung von alten Körben, die an einem Wäschegestell hängen.*
RECHTE SEITE: *Patricia hat die besondere Gabe, schlichte Gegenstände in Stilleben zu verwandeln. Das beweisen der Geranientopf und die Kieselsteine auf der Küchenfensterbank.*

A GAUCHE: *Dans la vieille cuisine, des chaises campagnardes Windsor, une table et un banc rustique et une collection de vieux paniers accrochés au sèche-linge créent une ambiance chaleureuse et accueillante.*
PAGE DE DROITE: *Patricia a le don de transformer l'objet le plus banal en nature morte: sur l'appui de fenêtre de la cuisine, un simple géranium en pot et quelques galets témoignent de son talent.*

LEFT: *Patricia loves vivid colours; she herself designed the elegant wooden wall-sofa in her linden-green drawing room, before decorating it with a Veronese-green "faux marbre" pattern.*
FACING PAGE: *In combining bright canary yellow with cornflower blue, Patricia perpetuated a time-honoured decorative tradition – yet she confesses that some of her friends and clients were greatly taken aback by the "daring" décor of her bedroom.*

LINKS: *Patricia mag lebhafte Farben. Sie hat auch die elegante Holzbank in dem lindgrünen Salon entworfen und später in Pistaziengrün marmorieren lassen.*
RECHTE SEITE: *Mit dem grellen Kanariengelb und knalligen Kornblumenblau greift*

Patricia eine lange Designtradition auf. Sie räumt jedoch ein, daß einige ihrer Freunde und Kunden auf die kühne Mischung im Schlafzimmer sprachlos reagierten.

A GAUCHE: *Patricia adore les couleurs vives et dans son salon vert tilleul elle a aussi dessiné la banquette en bois aux formes élégantes qu'elle a fait peindre ensuite en faux marbre vert Véronèse.*
PAGE DE DROITE: *En combinant un jaune canari criard avec un bleu barbeau très vif, Patricia poursuivait une longue tradition décorative, mais elle avoue que certains de ses amis et clients furent ébahis en voyant le décor audacieux de sa chambre à coucher.*

RIGHT: *Every room at Cedar Lodge has its own typically English cosy atmosphere – and to emphasise the relaxed feel of the décor, Patricia is quite happy to place a fine Victorian armchair next to a wickerwork garden chair.*

RECHTS: *Jedes der Zimmer von Cedar Lodge strahlt die typisch englische »cosyness« aus. Hier hat Patricia einen viktorianischen Sessel mit einem schlichten Gartenstuhl aus Korbgeflecht kombiniert.*

A DROITE: *Dans chaque pièce de Cedar Lodge règne une ambiance «cosy» typiquement anglaise, et pour accentuer le côté décontracté de la décoration Patricia n'a pas hésité à juxtaposer un fauteuil victorien et un fauteuil de jardin en osier.*

CHURCH COTTAGE
Sophie Hicks and Roddy Campbell
Northamptonshire

You reach Church Cottage after negotiating a number of gates and fields occupied by sheep. After this you see a small church, and then a large Queen Anne house comes into sight, along with the modest farmhouse which is the country retreat of the architect Sophie Hicks and her husband Roddy Campbell. Originally, Church Cottage was the kitchen and laundry for the big house and when Sophie and her family arrived they carried on where the former owner, Vanessa Williams-Ellis, had left off. Vanessa had saved the farmhouse from demolition, installed water and electricity, painted the walls with a linden-green wash, and refrained from touching the magnificent old floors. The contribution of the newcomers was equally minimal. Hicks, a former fashion editor of "Harpers and Queen" and "Vogue", confined herself to putting in a few kitchen units built with packing cases, while her husband laid out a vegetable garden and planted a box hedge around it. Assorted ethnic objects brought home from Sophie's travels around the world add a note or two of exoticism, but apart from these, everything in Church Cottage is "luxe, calme et volupté", as Baudelaire would put it.

In one of the bedrooms, Sophie kept intact the brick wall of the old dovecote.

In einem der Schlafzimmer hat Sophie die Ziegelsteinmauer des ehemaligen Taubenhauses belassen.

Dans une des chambres à coucher, Sophie a gardé intact le mur de briques de l'ancien pigeonnier.

At dusk, Church Cottage and the outline of the church beside it are enveloped in shadows and mystery.

Bei Einbruch der Dunkelheit versinken Church Cottage und die benachbarte Kirche in geheimnisvollen Schatten… die Gespensterstunde naht!

A la tombée du jour, Church Cottage et la silhouette de l'église adjacente s'enveloppent d'ombres et de mystère … c'est bientôt l'heure des fantômes!

Um nach Church Cottage zu gelangen, muß man erst einige Gatter und Wiesen mit grasenden Schafherden überwinden. Geht man dann an der kleinen Kirche entlang, die aus einem alten Gemälde stammen könnte, sieht man ein großes Steinhaus aus dem frühen 18. Jahrhundert und schließlich den einfachen Bauernhof, auf den sich die Architektin Sophie Hicks und ihr Mann Roddy Campbell zurückgezogen haben. Church Cottage hatte früher die Küche und Waschküche des Herrschaftshauses beherbergt. Als Sophie, Roddy und ihre Kinder sich hier niederließen, bewahrten sie gewissermaßen das Vermächtnis der vorherigen Eigentümerin Vanessa Williams-Ellis. Diese hatte den Hof vor dem Verfall gerettet, Wasser- und Stromleitungen legen lassen, die Wände der Innenräume in Lindgrün getüncht und die alten Dielenbohlen belassen. Die neuen Bewohner änderten deshalb nur wenig. Sophie Hicks, ehemaliger »Fashion Editor« von »Harpers & Queen« und »Vogue«, baute nur einige Küchenelemente aus ehemaligen Verpackungskisten ein, während ihr Mann einen Gemüsegarten mit Buchsbaumeinfassung anlegte. Die ethnischen Objekte sind Souvenirs von Sophies Fernreisen und bringen eine exotische Note in das Cottage. Ansonsten bietet Church Cottage nur »Luxus, Stille und Sinnlichkeit« – um mit Baudelaire zu sprechen.

On n'atteint Church Cottage qu'après avoir franchi plusieurs barrières et traversé des prés où paissent les moutons. Et puis, en passant devant une petite église qui semble sortie tout droit d'un tableau ancien, on aperçoit une grande maison en pierre de style Queen Anne du début du 18ᵉ siècle et la modeste ferme qui sert de retraite campagnarde à l'architecte Sophie Hicks et son mari Roddy Campbell. Church Cottage abritait jadis les cuisines et la buanderie de la demeure seigneuriale, et quand Sophie, Roddy et leurs enfants s'installèrent dans les lieux, ils reprirent en quelque sorte le flambeau de l'ancienne propriétaire Vanessa Williams-Ellis. Celle-ci avait sauvé la ferme de la démolition et, après avoir installé l'eau et l'électricité, s'était contentée de badigeonner les murs avec un lavis à la chaux vert tilleul, se gardant de toucher aux magnifiques sols anciens. L'apport des nouveaux habitants a été minime. Hicks – ancien «fashion editor» de «Harpers & Queen» et de «Vogue» – s'est limitée à installer quelques éléments de cuisine (construits avec des caisses d'emballage!) et son mari a créé un potager entouré d'une haie de buis. Des objets ethniques que Sophie a ramenés de ses voyages autour du monde, apportent une note d'exotisme, et pour le reste tout dans Church Cottage – citons Baudelaire – n'est que «luxe, calme et volupté».

In the sitting room, with its pure lines, a fire crackles in the hearth.

Im Salon mit den klaren Linien begrüßt ein knisterndes Holzfeuer die Besucher.

Dans le salon aux lignes épurées, une bonne flambée accueille les visiteurs.

LEFT: *The light-green walls form a pleasing contrast with the furniture, the neo-Gothic candelabrum and the cushion covered with a fabric from Indonesia.*
FACING PAGE: *In a corner of the sitting room is the strange apparition of the prow of a canoe from Papua New Guinea, and on the wall behind hangs a portrait of the great art patron Edward James by Cecil Beaton (1904–1980), with the caption "Good Dog Edward by Clever Bird Beaton".*

LINKS: *Die lindgrünen Wände bilden einen schönen Kontrast zu den Möbeln, dem neugotischen Kerzenständer und dem Kissen, das mit einem indonesischen Stoff bezogen ist.*
RECHTE SEITE: *In einer Ecke des Salons ragt der Bug eines Einbaums aus Papua empor. An der Wand befindet sich ein Porträt des Kunstmäzens Edward James, das Cecil Beaton (1904–1980) fotografiert hat. Die Inschrift besagt: »Good Dog Edward by Clever Bird Beaton«.*

A GAUCHE: *Les murs tilleul forment un contraste heureux avec les meubles, le chandelier néogothique et le coussin recouvert d'un tissu indonésien.*
PAGE DE DROITE: *Dans le salon se dresse une proue de pirogue papoue et sur le mur du fond un portrait du mécène Edward James – signé Cecil Beaton (1904–1980) – porte l'inscription: «Good Dog Edward by Clever Bird Beaton».*

LEFT: *On the first floor, a door opens into a bedroom with an armchair made of branches and pigskin from Taos, New Mexico.*
FACING PAGE: *There is nothing to distract the eye in this peaceful corner of the sitting room. The fireplace itself has become a work of art.*

LINKS: *In der oberen Etage führt eine Tür in ein Schlafzimmer mit einem Armlehnstuhl aus Ästen und Schweinsleder, der aus Taos in New Mexico stammt.*
RECHTE SEITE: *In dieser friedlichen Ecke des Salons lenkt nichts das Auge des Betrachters ab. So wird der Kamin zu einem Kunstwerk…*

A GAUCHE: *A l'étage, une porte s'ouvre sur une chambre à coucher et sur un fauteuil en branches et en peau de porc trouvé à Taos, Nouveau-Mexique.*
PAGE DE DROITE: *Rien ne vient distraire l'œil dans ce coin paisible du salon. La cheminée elle-même est devenue une œuvre d'art…*

"Straining my ears I could detect nothing but the old clock ticking loudly on the landing below me… I hurried down as quickly as the utter darkness permitted, holding on to the handrail of the banister. Once in the hall, I groped my way to the coat-hooks and found my overcoat. Pulling it on I cautiously opened the door and peered round it. There was a wind for the first time in several days and a few scattered flakes of snow were falling – or rather, blowing about."

»Als ich die Ohren spitzte, konnte ich nichts hören außer dem lauten Ticken der alten Uhr auf dem Treppenabsatz unter mir… Ich eilte so schnell herab, wie die Dunkelheit es zuließ, wobei ich mich am Geländer festhielt. Unten in der Halle tastete ich nach der Garderobe und fand meinen Übermantel. Ich streifte ihn über, öffnete vorsichtig die Tür und sah mich um. Zum ersten Mal seit Tagen ging ein Wind und vereinzelt fielen Schneeflocken herab, die der Wind umhertrieb.«

«Je dressai l'oreille mais n'entendis rien à part le tic-tac bruyant de la vieille horloge sur le palier du dessous… Je descendis aussi vite que le permettait l'obscurité totale en tenant la rampe de l'escalier. Arrivé dans le hall, j'avançai à tâtons jusqu'au portemanteaux et trouvai mon manteau. Je l'enfilai, j'ouvris prudemment la porte et scrutai les alentours. Il y avait du vent pour la première fois en quelques jours et quelques flocons de neige dispersés tombaient, ou plutôt volaient.»

CHARLES PALLISER
The Unburied

In the kitchen, Sophie has fashioned cupboards out of old packing crates. The kitchen table and the 18th-century-inspired chairs date from the 19th century, while the Aga cooker is a relic of the Thirties.

In der Küche hat Sophie aus alten Verpackungskisten Schränke gebaut. Der Küchentisch und die vom 18. Jahrhundert inspirierten Stühle stammen aus dem 19. Jahrhundert. Der Aga-Herd ist ein Relikt aus den dreißiger Jahren.

Dans la cuisine, Sophie a construit des armoires en se servant de vieilles caisses d'emballage. La table et les chaises d'inspiration 18ᵉ datent du 19ᵉ siècle et la cuisinière Aga est une relique des années trente.

ABOVE: *The bed, with its gate-like bedhead, was built from salvaged planks and posts by a friend of Sophie's. The counterpane is from India; the stripped pitch pine cupboard and the Windsor chair emphasise the rusticity of the room.*
RIGHT: *The padded Victorian armchair is covered with canvas.*
FACING PAGE: *The architect and her husband thought that the combination of pink stucco and splashes of limewash created an interesting decorative effect – so they left it that way.*

OBEN: *Das Bett mit einem Kopfteil in Form eines Gatters hat ein Freund von Sophie aus alten Brettern entworfen. Die Tagesdecke stammt aus Indien. Der Schrank aus gebeizter Pechkiefer und der Windsor-Stuhl betonen das rustikale Flair.*
RECHTS: *Der viktorianische Polstersessel erhielt einen Bezug aus grobem Leinen.*
RECHTE SEITE: *Die Hausbewohner fanden, daß die Kombination aus rosa Gips und Kalkspritzern einen hübschen Effekt auf den Wänden ergibt.*

CI-DESSUS: *Le lit avec sa tête de lit en forme de barrière a été construit avec des planches et des poteaux de récupération par un ami de Sophie. Le couvre-lit vient de l'Inde; l'armoire en pitchpin décapé et la chaise Windsor accentuent le côté rustique de l'ensemble.*
A DROITE: *Le fauteuil capitonné victorien a été recouvert de canevas.*
PAGE DE DROITE: *L'architecte et son mari ont trouvé que la combinaison du stuc rose et les éclaboussures de la chaux faisaient un bel effet sur les murs: ils ont décidé de le garder!*

WEST WYCOMBE PARK
Sir Francis Dashwood
Buckinghamshire

Benjamin Franklin, who was a frequent guest at West Wycombe Park, called the gardens there "a paradise". Should that great American return today for a ramble around the swan-shaped lake at Wycombe, he would find that little has changed: the bridges, waterfalls, temples, statues and mausoleum are still as they were, and so is the marvellous Palladian house itself, standing with its colonnades and porticos in the hollow of a valley surrounded by the rolling Chilterns. The house dates back to the 18th century, when it was built by Sir Francis Dashwood, the second baronet, later Lord Despencer. Sir Francis was much influenced in his aesthetic thinking by the Grand Tour he had made through the Low Countries, France, and Italy. On his return to England he resolved to transform his family seat into a masterpiece of Palladian fantasy, enlisting the architects Roger Morris, John Donowell and Nicholas Revett to plan and carry out the work. The Dashwood family still lives amid the sumptuous interiors and magnificent ceilings painted by Giuseppe Borgnis in the mid-18th century. Since 1943 they have received help from the National Trust in preserving this jewel of unearthly romantic beauty.

A splendid white marble sphinx graces the garden with its serene presence.

Eine ernste, weiße Marmor-Sphinx im Garten.

Une splendide sphinge en marbre blanc orne le jardin de sa présence sereine.

Benjamin Franklin, der hier häufig zu Besuch war, nannte die Gärten von West Wycombe Park ein »Paradies«. Wenn er zurückkehren und wieder um den schwanenförmigen Teich spazieren könnte, würde er feststellen, daß sich nichts verändert hat: weder die Brücken, noch die Wasserfälle oder Tempel, das Mausoleum oder die Statuen. Und auch das palladianische Haus mit den Säulengängen und den von der Antike inspirierten Säulenhallen steht noch in dem kleinen Tal in der hügeligen Landschaft von Chiltern. Die Erhaltung des Gebäudes, dessen Ursprünge bis ins 18. Jahrhundert zurückreichen, ist weitgehend dem Engagement von Sir Francis Dashwood zu verdanken, des zweiten Baronnet und zukünftigen Lord Le Despencer, dessen Geschmack von einer »Grand Tour« durch Holland, Frankreich und besonders Italien geprägt wurde. Er verwandelte das Haus seiner Vorfahren mit Hilfe einer Heerschar von begabten Architekten, wie Roger Morris, John Donowell und Nicholas Revett, in ein wahres Meisterwerk des palladianischen Klassizismus. Zwei Jahrhunderte nach der Grundsteinlegung von West Wycombe Park ist das Haus mit den herrlichen Räumen und den Mitte des 18. Jahrhunderts von Giuseppe Borgnis bemalten Decken immer noch im Besitz der Dashwoods. Seit 1943 beteiligt sich der National Trust an der Konservierung dieses Juwels, dessen zeitlose Schönheit jede romantische Seele begeistert.

The Ionic east portico is flanked by a pair of marble lions inspired by antiquity.

Die ionischen Säulen der Eingangshalle im Osten werden flankiert von einem marmornen, antikisierenden Löwenpaar.

Le portique est –de style ionique – est flanqué d'une paire de lions en marbre inspirés de l'antiquité.

Benjamin Franklin, qui était un invité fréquent, trouvait que les jardins de West Wycombe Park étaient un vrai paradis; s'il pouvait revenir se promener aujourd'hui autour du lac en forme de cygne, il verrait que rien n'a changé: ni les ponts, ni les cascades, ni les temples, ni le mausolée et les statues, ni la merveilleuse maison palladienne, avec ses colonnades et ses portiques inspirés du monde antique, plantée au milieu d'un vallon et entourée du paysage aux courbes douces des collines du Chiltern. La maison, dont les origines remontent au 18e siècle, fut en grande partie l'œuvre de Sir Francis Dashwood, le second baronnet et futur Lord Le Despencer, qui, influencé esthétiquement par son Grand Tour des Pays-Bas, de la France et – surtout – de l'Italie, transforma la maison de ses ancêtres en véritable chef-d'œuvre palladien, assisté par une pléiade d'architectes parmi lesquels nous citerons Roger Morris, John Donowell et Nicholas Revett. Deux siècles après la création de West Wycombe Park, la maison aux intérieurs somptueux et aux magnifiques plafonds peints par Giuseppe Borgnis au milieu du 18e siècle est toujours la demeure des Dashwood; le National Trust les aide, depuis 1943, à préserver ce joyau dont la beauté intemporelle continue d'enchanter les âmes romantiques.

West Wycombe Park sits like a precious stone in its setting of green Buckinghamshire hills.

West Wycombe Park liegt wie ein Juwel eingebettet in die sattgrünen Hügel von Buckinghamshire.

West Wycombe Park a été posé, tel un joyau précieux, au creux d'un vallon du Buckinghamshire entouré de collines verdoyantes.

LEFT: *This head of a Roman emperor has not moved from its plinth since it was placed here over 200 years ago.*
FACING PAGE: *view of the impressive ground-floor colonnade. The gallery is in the purest classical style, ending in a portico decorated with statuary, which is, notwithstanding, a trompe l'œil. The busts aligned against the wall emphasise its length.*

LINKS: *Der Kopf eines römischen Kaisers ruht seit mehr als zwei Jahrhunderten auf einem Sockel aus falschem Marmor.*
RECHTE SEITE: *Blick in den eindrucksvollen Säulengang im Erdgeschoß. Die in bester klassizistischer Tradition gestaltete Galerie mündet in eine mit Statuen dekorierte Säulenhalle, die allerdings eine »Trompe l'œil«-Malerei darstellt. Die längs der Wand aufgestellten Büsten betonen die perspektivische Tiefe.*

A GAUCHE: *Cette tête d'empereur romain n'a pas quitté son socle en faux marbre depuis plus de deux siècles.*
PAGE DE DROITE: *la colonnade impressionnante du rez-de-chaussée. La galerie, dans la meilleure tradition classique, se termine par un portique décoré de statuaire qui est cependant un trompe-l'œil. Les bustes alignés le long du mur accentuent l'étendue de la construction.*

RIGHT: *a bust of Hercules in a corner of the colonnade.*

RECHTS: *Eine Herkules-Büste schmückt eine Ecke des Säulengangs.*

A DROITE: *Un buste d'Hercule orne un coin de la colonnade.*

LEFT: *The drawing rooms of West Wycombe Park are filled with treasures accumulated by generations of Dashwoods.*
FACING PAGE: *The dining room, with its sunflower yellow walls, neoclassical fireplace and restrained Georgian furniture.*

LINKS: *Die Salons von West Wycombe Park sind prall gefüllt mit Schätzen, die die Dashwoods über Generationen hinweg angesammelt haben.*
RECHTE SEITE: *der Speisesaal mit den sonnenblumengelben Wänden, dem neoklassizistischen Kamin und den schlichten Möbeln aus der Zeit von George III.*

A GAUCHE: *Les salons de West Wycombe Park regorgent de trésors accumulés par des générations de Dashwood.*
PAGE DE DROITE: *La salle à manger avec ses murs jaune tournesol, sa cheminée néoclassique et son mobilier George III aux lignes sobres.*

RIGHT: *a buttercup-yellow silk cushion on a Georgian English armchair.*
FAR RIGHT: *a grotesque "mascherone", detail of the décor of a William and Mary table dating from the late 17th century.*

RECHTS: *Ein Kissen mit einem Bezug aus butterblumengelber Seide liegt auf einem georgianischen Sessel.*

GANZ RECHTS: *Eine groteske Maske ziert eine Konsole im William-and-Mary-Stil aus dem späten 17. Jahrhundert.*

A DROITE: *Un coussin en soie bouton d'or a été posé sur un fauteuil anglais de l'époque georgienne.*
A L'EXTRÊME DROITE: *Un «mascherone» grotesque et grimaçant orne une console de l'époque William and Mary de la fin du 17e siècle.*

On the broad landing of the first floor, Ionic columns standing in the foreground accentuate the gracefulness of a statue of Venus in white marble.

Die ionischen Säulen auf dem breiten Treppenabsatz zum ersten Stock heben die zeitlose Anmut der Venusstatue aus weißem Marmor hervor.

Sur le vaste palier du premier étage, des colonnes ioniques forment une avant-scène qui met en valeur la grâce intemporelle d'une Vénus en marbre blanc.

LEFT: *In Lady Dash-
wood's bedroom, the
delicate pastel tones of
the walls and fabrics
combine with the 18th-
century four-poster bed
to strike a dainty,
intensely feminine note.*
FACING PAGE: *a
porcelain vase converted
into a lamp, decorated
with a charming plump
cherub.*

LINKS: *Das Himmel-
bett aus dem 18. Jahr-
hundert und die zart
abgestuften Pastelltöne
der Wände und Stoffe
im Schlafzimmer der
Lady Dashwood geben
dem Raum eine beson-
ders feminine Note.*
RECHTE SEITE: *Die
zur Lampe umfunktio-
nierte Porzellanvase ist
mit einem triumphie-
renden pausbäckigen
Putto verziert.*

A GAUCHE: *Dans la
chambre à coucher de
Lady Dashwood, les
délicats tons pastels des
murs et des tissus et le lit
à baldaquin 18ᵉ, appor-
tent une note de fragilité
et de féminité.*
PAGE DE DROITE:
*Un vase en porcelaine
transformé en lampe a
été décoré d'une scène
charmante représentant
un chérubin joufflu et
triomphant.*

HYDE HALL BARN
Mark Brazier-Jones
Hertfordshire

During the Eighties, the London designers Tom Dixon, André Dubreuil and Mark Brazier-Jones took the world of design by storm with their decorative metal furniture and objects. Very soon people were talking about a "school" which drew its inspiration directly from nature and which distinguished itself from the fashionable "high-tech" of the moment by introducing sinuous plant forms and outlines modelled on the shapes of animals. The work of Brazier-Jones, which included objects like winged chairs, lamps decorated with glass and crystal droplets, and a chaise longue with dangerous-looking clawed feet, was a huge success with lovers of good design, and his pieces were bought by some of the world's most sophisticated collectors. Born in New Zealand, Brazier-Jones later found the means to get away from the world and work in complete tranquillity when he bought an old barn at Buntingford in Hertfordshire. The building, which is set in a landscape of rolling hills, combines a workshop that looks like Vulcan's forge with a place to live that is a cross between a gipsy encampment and a chaotic hippie pad. It supplies the perfect backdrop for Brazier-Jones's own creations, with such visual delights as wrought-iron baroque furniture and a wrought-iron bed draped with Indian fabrics.

Detail of the front door, made by Mark Brazier-Jones.

Detail des von Mark Brazier-Jones entworfenen großen Eingangstores.

Un détail de la grande porte d'entrée créée par Mark Brazier-Jones.

In den achtziger Jahren eroberten die jungen Londoner Designer Tom Dixon, André Dubreuil und Mark Brazier-Jones mit ihren Möbeln und dekorativen Objekten aus Metall die Designwelt. Schon bald sprach man von einer neuen »Schule«, die sich deutlich vom High-Tech-Trend abhob und statt dessen an der Natur mit ihren verschlungenen vegetabilen Formen und morphologischen Strukturen orientierte. Besonders die Entwürfe von Mark Brazier-Jones – seine Flügelsessel, seine mit dicken Glastropfen verzierten Leuchtkörper und seine Chaiselongue mit Füßen in Form von aggressiven Tierkrallen – faszinierten die Designfans und sind heute gesuchte Sammlerstücke. Als der gebürtige Neuseeländer Brazier-Jones einen ruhigen Winkel suchte, um in Ruhe arbeiten zu können, ließ er sich in einer alten Scheune bei Buntingford in Hertfordshire nieder. Sein Atelier erinnert an die Schmiede des Vulkans, die Wohnung dagegen ist eine Mischung aus dem Loft eines Bohème-Künstlers und einer chaotischen Hippieabsteige. Das »Haus« ist der perfekte Rahmen für seine Kreationen und bietet überraschende visuelle Effekte, wie etwa einige barocke Möbel und ein schmiedeeisernes Bett mit einer Tagesdecke aus indischen Stoffen. Die Landschaft um Hyde Hall Barn prägen sanfte Hügel, vom Wind gekrümmte Bäume und ein oft wolkenverhangener Himmel.

Mark Brazier-Jones with one of his latest creations.

Mark Brazier-Jones mit einem seiner neuesten Entwürfe.

Mark Brazier-Jones avec une de ses dernières créations.

Dans les années quatre vingt, les jeunes créateurs londoniens Tom Dixon, André Dubreuil et Mark Brazier-Jones conquirent le monde du design avec leur mobilier et leurs objets décoratifs en métal et, très vite, on commença à parler d'un «école» qui s'inspirait directement de la nature et se distinguait nettement du high-tech en vogue en introduisant des formes végétales sinueuses et des silhouettes copiées sur la morphologie des animaux. En ce qui concerne l'œuvre de Mark Brazier-Jones, ses sièges dotés d'ailes, ses luminaires ornés de grosses gouttes de verre et de cristal et sa chaise longue perchée sur des pattes aux griffes agressives, ne laissèrent pas indifférents les fanatiques du design. Depuis, la production de Brazier-Jones se voit arrachée par les collectionneurs les plus sophistiqués. L'artiste, né en Nouvelle-Zélande, a trouvé un refuge pour travailler en toute tranquillité: il s'est installé dans une vieille grange du côté de Buntingford dans le Hertfordshire. Combinant un atelier qui ressemble à la forge de Vulcain et un logis qui tient à la fois du gîte bohémien et du repère d'un hippie chaotique, sa «maison» est le décor parfait pour ses propres créations, et pour la surprise visuelle de quelques meubles baroques et d'un lit en fer forgé drapé de tissus indiens. Au-delà de Hyde Hall Barn, il y a la campagne avec son paysage de douces collines, ses arbres tordus et son ciel souvent lourd de nuages.

Even in the worst winter weather, the English landscape casts a spell.

Sogar an sehr trüben Wintertagen übt die englische Landschaft einen eigenartigen Reiz aus.

Même en hiver et par le temps le plus maussade, le paysage anglais continue d'exercer un certain charme.

LEFT: *In the small
kitchen – built by Mark
at minimal expense with
maximum imagination
– even the chair and
candlesticks were made
by him.*
FACING PAGE: *On a
piece of furniture used
for storing files, Brazier-
Jones has assembled
an assortment of his
favourite objects. Pro-
tected by Victorian bell
jars, a peculiar object
made several years ago
and a human skull
reveal Mark's taste for
the bizarre.*

LINKS: *Stuhl und
Kerzenständer in der
eher kleinen Küche, die
Mark mit wenig Mit-
teln und viel Phantasie
eingerichtet hat, sind
Schöpfungen des Haus-
herrn.*
RECHTE SEITE: *Auf
dieser Kommode hat
Brazier-Jones einige sei-
ner Lieblingsgegenstände
arrangiert. Viktoriani-
sche Glasstürze beschir-
men ein ungewöhnliches
Objekt, das er vor eini-
gen Jahren entworfen
hat, sowie einen mensch-
lichen Schädel.*

A GAUCHE: *Dans la
cuisine aux dimensions
modestes que Mark a
construite avec peu de
moyens et beaucoup
d'imagination, la chaise
et les bougeoirs portent
sa signature.*
PAGE DE DROITE:
*Sur un meuble à
archives, Brazier-Jones a
rassemblé quelques-uns
de ses objets favoris.
Protégés par des globes
victoriens, un objet inso-
lite créé il y a quelques
années et un crâne
humain révèlent le goût
de Mark pour le bizarre.*

ASTROCHARGER/WINGED C/STICK.

CABIN

ST. IA

LEFT: *Mark is fond of richly-embroidered fabrics bought in India, and he strews them freely around his house.*
FACING PAGE: *In the psychedelic-looking bedroom, a wildly baroque Italian chair, an Art Deco electric radiator in the shape of a sailing boat, and a hanging lamp by Brazier-Jones stand out against a wall covered in symbols and graffiti. The painting on the right also bears his signature.*

LINKS: *Mark mag reich bestickte indische Stoffe, und er verwendet sie großzügig.*
RECHTE SEITE: *In dem psychedelisch anmutenden Schlafzimmer befinden sich ein sehr barocker italienischer Sessel, ein elektrischer Art-Deco-Heizkörper in Form eines Segelschiffs und eine von Brazier-Jones entworfene Hängelampe vor der mit Graffitis und Symbolen übersäten Wand. Auch das rechte Gemälde stammt von Mark.*

A GAUCHE: *Mark adore les tissus richement brodés chinés en Inde, et il les emploie généreusement.*
PAGE DE DROITE: *Dans la chambre à coucher d'apparence «psychédélique», un fauteuil italien follement baroque, un radiateur électrique Art Déco en forme de voilier et une suspension signée Brazier-Jones se détachent sur un mur parsemé de graffitis et de symboles. Le tableau à droite est une œuvre de Mark.*

"*The landscape through which the path runs is very beautiful brown heathland with birches and pine trees here and there and patches of yellow sand, and in the distance the mountains against the sun. Truly, it is not a picture but an inspiration…*"

»*Die Landschaft, durch die der Weg führt, ist so schön, brauner Heideboden, hier und da Birken und Kiefern und Flecken von gelbem Sand, und in der Ferne, gegen die Sonne, Berge. Eigentlich ist es kein Bild, sondern eine Inspiration…*«

«*Le paysage que traverse le chemin est très beau, des landes brunes avec des bouleaux et des pins ici et là et des plaques de sable jaune, et au loin, les montagnes contre le soleil. Vraiment, ce n'est pas une image mais une inspiration…*»

VINCENT VAN GOGH
Letter to his brother Theo describing the countryside near Isleworth · Beschreibung der Landschaft bei Isleworth in einem Brief an seinen Bruder Theo · Lettre à son frère Théo décrivant le paysage près d'Isleworth

THE BOAT HOUSE
Helen Oxenbury and John Burningham
Suffolk

From a distance, the wooden house painted bright blue and white looks like a fishing boat that has foundered on the bank of a river as it flows into the North Sea. The closer you get to the site – which, being right on the estuary, is indeed pretty vulnerable as a place to live – the stronger this impression grows. Twelve years ago John Burningham and Helen Oxenbury, a couple who make their living by writing and illustrating children's books and who have become world famous in the process, discovered the Boat House on one of the easternmost points of the Suffolk coast. They fell in love with it immediately. The Boat House, formerly used for storing boats, as its name suggests, was surrounded by a jumble of rowboats, and built right on the water. Helen, who grew up in this part of the world and who has described it in her best-selling book "We're Going On A Bear Hunt", was deliriously happy to be back among the sights and sounds of her girlhood – water slapping at the shore, shifting skies, boats coming and going along the river. Today, thanks to John's muscular enthusiasm for the task of adding a second floor with picture windows, a pinewood spiral staircase, and a Gustavian-style stove with a frieze of Delft tiles, she can congratulate herself on possessing a house that is every bit as magical as those she describes for her young readers.

John built the Swedish stove using large white tiles. The frieze of ships is in Delft earthenware.

John hat den schwedischen Ofen mit großen weißen Kacheln neu verkleidet. Der mit Schiffen verzierte Fries besteht aus Delfter Fayence.

John a revêtu le poêle suédois de grands carreaux blancs. La frise décorée de navires anciens est en faïence de Delft.

The Boat House seems to float at the extreme limit of dry land, where the estuary broadens and the river meets the North Sea.

Einem Kahn vergleich-bar treibt The Boat House an der äußersten Spitze des Festlandes, dort wo der Fluß in die Nordsee mündet.

Telle une barque, le Boat House flotte sur la pointe extrême de la terre ferme, là où l'estuaire s'élargit pour devenir mer du Nord.

Von weitem könnte man das strahlend blau-weiß lackierte Holzhaus für ein Fischerboot halten, das am Ufer eines in die Nordsee mündenden Flußes gestrandet ist. Die gefährlich dichte Lage direkt an der Mündung verstärkt diesen Eindruck beim Näherkommen noch. Die weltberühmten Kinderbuch-autoren und -illustratoren Helen Oxenbury und John Bur-ningham verliebten sich vor zwölf Jahren in The Boat House. Sie waren sofort begeistert von dem alten Bootshaus an einem der äußersten Punkte der Küste von Suffolk, um das herum unzählige Boote plätschernd im Wasser schaukeln. Helen, die in der Region aufgewachsen ist und später von dieser Land-schaft zu dem Buch »Wir gehen auf Bärenjagd« inspiriert wur-de, war glücklich, schöne Kindheitserinnerungen wiederzufin-den: das Klatschen der Wellen, den sich ständig verändernden Himmel und das Kommen und Gehen der Kähne und Schiffe. Dem Enthusiasmus und den »Muskeln« von John – der eine Etage mit Sprossenfenstern, einer Wendeltreppe aus hellem Holz und einem Fayence-Ofen im »Gustavian-Style« mit Delfter Kachelleiste anbaute – ist es zu verdanken, daß das Paar heute eines jener magischen Häuser besitzt, die sich Helen schon so oft für ihre kleinen Leser ausgedacht hat…

The door is painted Mediterranean blue as an antidote to grey, sun-less east coast days.

Um an sonnenarmen Tagen keinen Trübsinn aufkommen zu lassen, wurde die Tür in medi-terran anmutendem Meerblau gestrichen.

La porte a été peinte en bleu méditerranéen afin de chasser la grisaille des longues journées sans soleil.

De loin, la maison de bois peinte en blanc et en bleu vif, res-semble à un bateau de pêcheur échoué sur les bords d'une rivière qui mène à la mer du Nord. Quand on s'approche, sa position – risquée – au ras de l'estuaire, ne fait qu'accentuer cette illusion. Il y a douze ans que John Burningham et Helen Oxenbury, auteurs et illustrateurs de livres d'enfants de renom-mée mondiale, ont découvert le Boat House et ils se sont tout de suite épris de cette ancienne remise à bateaux entourée d'une multitude de chaloupes et qui «faisait trempette», sur une des pointes les plus extrêmes de la côte de Suffolk. Helen, qui a grandi dans la région et qui devait s'inspirer plus tard du paysage en illustrant son livre à grand succès «We're Going on a Bear Hunt», était ravie de retrouver ses tendres souvenirs d'enfance, le clapotis de l'eau, le ciel capricieux et le va-et-vient des barques et des bateaux. Aujourd'hui, grâce à l'enthousias-me et aux «muscles» de John – il a enrichi le Boat House d'un étage équipé de fenêtres à lanterne, d'un escalier en colimaçon en bois blond et d'un poêle en faïence de style gustavien orné d'une frise en carrelage de Delft –, elle peut se vanter de possé-der une maison qui ressemble aux demeures enchantées qu'elle imagine si souvent pour ses petits lecteurs…

LEFT: *The wing chair came as a gift with the purchase of the house. John and Helen kept it "because it went so well with the lifebuoy".*
FACING PAGE: *By adding a second storey on top of the building, the owners created a room flooded with light which could also serve as an observatory. John took care of every detail, right down to the elegant window fittings.*

LINKS: *Der Ohrensessel war im Kaufpreis des Hauses inbegriffen. John und Helen haben ihn behalten, weil er so gut zu dem Rettungsring paßt!*
RECHTE SEITE: *Indem sie auf das ehemalige Bootshaus eine weitere Etage aufsetzten, gewannen die Eigentümer einen lichtdurchfluteten Raum hinzu, den man auch gut als »Observatorium« nutzen kann. John kümmerte sich auch um die kleinsten Details wie die elegant geformten Fenstergriffe.*

A GAUCHE: *Le fauteuil à oreilles vint en cadeau avec l'achat du maison. John et Helen l'ont gardé parce qu'il allait si bien avec la bouée de sauvetage!*
PAGE DE DROITE: *En surélevant l'ancienne remise à bateaux d'un étage, les habitants ont gagné une pièce baignée de lumière qui fait aussi office d'observatoire. John a fait attention au moindre détail, en témoigne la forme élégante des fermetures de fenêtre.*

LEFT: *The rattan arm-
chair in the entrance is
an original Lloyd Loom
piece, and the geranium-
red wardrobe is a hybrid
dating from the Thirties.*
FACING PAGE: *John
bought the spiral stair-
case at an auction in
Sussex, but he is firmly
convinced that it was
made in Austria or
Switzerland. The rattan
chair is from the Twen-
ties and the trousseau
trunk under the window
is dated 1746.*

LINKS: *Der Korbsessel
im Eingangsbereich ist
ein Original von Lloyd
Loom und das rote
Schränkchen ein zweck-
entfremdetes Möbel aus
den dreißiger Jahren.*
RECHTE SEITE: *John
erwarb die Wendeltreppe
in einem Auktionshaus
in Sussex, aber er ist
überzeugt, daß die Trep-
pe ursprünglich aus der
Schweiz oder Österreich
stammt. Der Korbliege-
stuhl stammt aus den
zwanziger Jahren, und
die Hochzeitstruhe unter
dem Fenster trägt die
Jahreszahl 1746.*

A GAUCHE: *Le fauteuil
en rotin dans l'entrée
est un Lloyd Loom d'ori-
gine et l'armoire rouge
géranium est un meuble
«hybride» datant des
années trente.*
PAGE DE DROITE:
*John a acheté l'escalier en
colimaçon dans une salle
de vente du Sussex mais
il est persuadé que cette
construction aux traits
«alpins» est originaire de
Suisse ou d'Autriche. Le
siège en rotin date des
années vingt et le coffre
de mariage, sous la fe-
nêtre, porte la date 1746.*

ABOVE AND RIGHT:
*The windows of the
raised living room offer
a panoramic view across
the estuary. The worn
garden furniture, the old
sofa and the Thirties
lamp evoke the relaxed
atmosphere of a real hol-
iday home.*
FACING PAGE: *There
is no more delightful
place to spend a weekend
than the Boat House. A
chaise longue covered in
flowered chintz, in com-
pany with an old
Moroccan tea table
beside the Burningham
stove – what better place
to relax?*

OBEN UND RECHTS:
*Die Fenster des oben
gelegenen Wohnzimmers
bieten einen Rundblick
über die Bucht. Die
gebrauchten Gartenmö-
bel, das alte Sofa und die
Lampe aus den dreißiger
Jahren vermitteln das
entspannte Flair eines
Ferienhauses.*
RECHTE SEITE: *Es
gibt nichts Angenehme-
res als ein Wochenende
in The Boat House. Die
mit geblümten Chintz
bezogene Chaiselongue
und ein alter marokka-
nischer Teetisch bilden
eine Ruheecke neben
dem von John angefer-
tigten Kachelofen.*

CI-DESSUS ET A
DROITE : *Les fenêtres
du séjour surélevé
offrent une vue panora-
mique sur l'estuaire. Le
mobilier de jardin usé,
le vieux canapé et la
lampe années trente
évoquent l'ambiance
nonchalante d'une vraie
maison de vacances.*
PAGE DE DROITE :
*Rien de plus agréable
qu'un week-end passé
dans le Boat House.
Une chaise longue
recouverte d'un chintz
fleuri et une vieille table
à thé marocaine for-
ment un coin-repos près
du poêle gustavien signé
Burningham.*

FACING PAGE: *In the
kitchen, a pretty old
dresser filled with
flower-patterned plates
– and exactly the right
mugs for good strong
workman's tea.*
ABOVE: *Everything is
kept simple in this liv-
ing room-dining room-
annexe: the rustic
straw-bottomed chairs,
the paper lantern and
the country table with
its check tablecloth.*
RIGHT: *Even though
the English coast is not
renowned for its clement
weather, the occupants
of the Boat House have
optimistically installed
a small open terrace.*

LINKE SEITE: *Eine
alte Anrichte in der ein-
fachen Küche ist prall
gefüllt mit geblümten
Tellern und den unver-
meidlichen »Tea Mugs«.*
OBEN: *Das Wohnzim-
mer, das gleichzeitig als
Eßzimmer dient, ist
einfach gehalten: rusti-
kale Stühle, eine Japan-
lampe und ein solider
Tisch mit karierter
Decke.*
RECHTS: *Obwohl die
englische Küste nicht
gerade für ständigen
Sonnenschein bekannt
ist, haben die Bewohner
von The Boat House
eine kleine Terrasse
angelegt.*

PAGE DE GAUCHE:
*Dans la modeste cui-
sine, un joli buffet
ancien accueille les
assiettes fleuries et les
«tea-mugs».*
CI-DESSUS: *Tout est
simple dans ce séjour-
salle à manger: les
chaises rustiques paillées,
le lampion en papier et
la table rustique couver-
te d'une nappe à car-
reaux.*
A DROITE: *Même si la
côte anglaise n'est pas
renommée pour son
temps invariablement
radieux, les habitants du
Boat House ont installé
une petite terrasse ouver-
te à tous les éléments.*

ℒOUDHAM HALL
Keith Skeel

Suffolk

The English dealer Keith Skeel began specialising in the sale of out-of-the-ordinary antiques several decades ago. Beyond his deep interest in what he calls "eccentricities", over the years he has acquired a passion for unusual houses. Loudham Hall – built around 1700 as the country seat of the Earl of Southampton, one of Charles II's illegitimate sons – was one pearl that Skeel yearned to have in his crown. He duly bought Loudham, a substantial red-brick Palladian building, and since the place did not entirely satisfy his craving for extravagance he set out to redecorate it completely. Those who know Keith understand that his notorious lack of patience can sometimes work miracles; by unleashing a crew of artisans on Loudham he managed in the space of a few months to transform the enormous reception rooms and their dingy décors into the purest "Skeel". The old surfaces were covered in eggshell finish paint, while the new owner was turning his London storehouses upside down in his search for "accessories like four-poster beds, period sofas, looking glasses, paintings, silver, china and old books". The result has been the metamorphosis of Loudham into a warm, welcoming and above all charming country home.

ABOVE: *the service entrance leading to the kitchen areas.*
LEFT: *In the pantry, an old baker's rack is crammed with storage containers of all shapes and sizes and from different periods.*

OBEN: *Der Dienstboteneingang führt direkt in die Küche.*
LINKS: *Ein ehemaliges Bäckerregal in der Speisekammer ist mit Vorratsbehältnissen in verschiedenen Formen und aus verschiedenen Epochen gefüllt.*

CI-DESSUS: *l'entrée de service qui mène tout droit aux cuisines.*
A GAUCHE: *Dans l'office, une ancienne étagère de boulanger est remplie de boîtes à provision de formes et d'époques variées.*

Vor einigen Jahrzehnten spezialisierte sich der englische Antiquitätenhändler Keith Skeel auf ausgefallene Objekte. Über das große Interesse für »Exzentrisches« hinaus entwickelte er auch eine Vorliebe für ungewöhnliche Häuser. Loudham Hall – das ehemalige »Landhaus« des Earl of Southhampton, einer der illegitimen Söhne von Charles II. – ist ein hinreißendes Juwel von ungefähr 1700, dem Skeel unmöglich widerstehen konnte. Doch da das imposante palladianische Gebäude aus rotem Ziegelstein seinen luxuriösen Ansprüchen nicht ganz genügte, beschloß er, das Innere komplett neu zu gestalten. Alle diejenigen, die Keith kennen, wissen, daß er mit seiner notorischen Ungeduld wahre Wunder bewirken kann. So waren sie nicht erstaunt, als Keith eine ganze Truppe von Handwerkern auf seinem neuen Besitz zusammentrommelte, die innerhalb von wenigen Monaten die verblaßten Interieurs der weitläufigen Salons in puren »Skeel« verwandelten. In Windeseile verpaßten sie den verblichenen Wänden einen eierschalenfarbenen neuen Anstrich. Unterdessen plünderte der Hausherrr seine Lager in London und brachte einige »Accessoires« nach Suffolk. Himmelbetten, antike Sofas, Spiegel, Gemälde, Silberbesteck, Porzellan und alte Bücher verwandelten Loudham Hall in ein einladendes Haus voll Charme und Wärme.

Keith Skeel loves parties and displays – and for him no party is complete without a balloon flight over the property.

Keith Skeel schätzt Luxus und Feste. Für ihn gehört zu einem Fest auch eine Fahrt im Heißluftballon!

Keith Skeel adore le faste et les fêtes et, pour lui, qui dit fête dit aussi un tour du domaine en montgolfière!

Il y a quelques décennies déjà que l'antiquaire anglais Keith Skeel se spécialise dans la vente d'antiquités hors du commun et, en dehors de son intérêt aigu pour les «eccentricities», il nourrit aussi une véritable passion pour les demeures exceptionnelles. Loudham Hall – à l'origine «la maison de campagne» du Earl of Southhampton, un des fils illégitimes du roi Charles II – était une perle qui ne pouvait manquer à la couronne de Skeel, mais comme la demeure imposante en briques rouges, construite vers 1700 dans le plus pur goût palladien, ne satisfaisait pas tout à fait son penchant pour le faste, il décida de la redécorer entièrement. Ceux qui connaissent Keith savent que son impatience notoire peut faire des miracles: on ne s'étonnera donc pas du fait qu'il ait «lâché» toute une équipe d'artisans sur sa nouvelle propriété et que ceux-ci ont transformé en quelques mois à peine ces vastes salons et leurs intérieurs défraîchis en du «Skeel» le plus pur, couvrant les patines anciennes d'une tornade de peinture coquille d'œuf. Pendant ce temps, le maître de maison dévalisait ses dépôts londoniens pour s'emparer de quelques accessoires tels que des lits à baldaquin, des canapés d'époque, des miroirs, des tableaux, de l'argenterie, de la porcelaine et des livres anciens qui allaient transformer Loudham Hall en une maison chaleureuse, accueillante et pleine de charme.

Near the woodshed, terracotta statues inspired by classical originals await their placement in the garden.

Neben den Holzvorräten warten einige antikisierende Statuen aus Terrakotta auf einen würdigeren Platz im Garten.

Près de la réserve de bois, des statues en terre cuite d'inspiration classique attendent une place de choix dans le jardin.

FACING PAGE: *a tho-
roughly British coat
rack, featuring hat,
skates, satchel and
umbrella in a single
spontaneous still life.*
RIGHT: *In the service
entrance, newspapers
and magazines await
the butler's iron. Visitors
are requested to sit on
the bench while awai-
ting admittance to
Keith's inner sanctum.*

LINKE SEITE: *Gibt es
ein typisch englischeres
Bild, als dieses zufällige
Garderoben-Stilleben
aus Hut, Schlittschu-
hen, Schulranzen und
Regenschirm?*
RECHTS: *Am Dienst-
boteneingang warten
die Zeitungen und Zeit-
schriften darauf, vom
Butler »glattgebügelt«
zu werden. Besucher
werden gebeten, auf der
Bank zu warten, bis sie
ins »Inner Sanctum«
von Keith Skeel vorge-
lassen werden…*

PAGE DE GAUCHE:
*Quoi de plus «british»
qu'un portemanteau
anglais où le chapeau,
les patins, le cartable et
le parapluie forment
une nature morte
spontanée?*
A DROITE: *Dans l'en-
trée de service, les jour-
naux et les magazines
attendent le coup de fer
du «butler». Les visi-
teurs sont priés de
prendre place sur la
banquette en attendant
d'être admis dans le
«inner sanctum» de
Monsieur Skeel.*

LEFT: *Keith Skeel has a remarkable knack for breathing new life into old kitchens whose shelves once groaned with provisions.*
FACING PAGE: *Baskets used by grape harvesters in France, a witchball from a Victorian garden, a rack of shelves from a pastry-shop, chinoiserie tea tins and 19th-century rustic furniture have all found their way to Loudham Hall.*

LINKS: *Keith Skeel besitzt die unfehlbare Gabe, die Atmosphäre von alten Küchen wieder aufleben zu lassen.*
RECHTE SEITE: *Französische Winzerkörbe, eine Hexenkugel aus einem viktorianischen Garten, ein Konditorei-Regal, mit Chinoiserien verzierte Teedosen aus Blech und rustikale Möbel aus dem 19. Jahrhundert fanden den Weg nach Loudham Hall.*

A GAUCHE: *Keith Skeel a un talent infaillible pour faire revivre les vieilles cuisines avec leurs étagères remplies de provisions.*
PAGE DE DROITE: *Des paniers de vignerons français, un «witchball» provenant d'un jardin victorien, une étagère de pâtissier, des boîtes à thé en tôle style «chinoiserie» et un mobilier rustique datant du 19e siècle ont tous trouvé le chemin de Loudham Hall.*

ABOVE: *"Still life with Fruits and a Grass-hopper" by Ambrosius Bosschaert the Younger (c. 1635–1640), private collection.*

OBEN: *»Früchtestilleben mit Heuschrecke« von Ambrosius Bosschaert dem Jüngeren (um 1635–1640), Privatbesitz.*

CI-DESSUS: *«Nature morte avec des fruits et une sauterelle» de Ambrosius Bosschaert le Jeune (vers 1635–1640), collection particulière.*

FACING PAGE: *In a little while, the china bowl will be emptied into a baking dish and its contents transformed into a crusty, sweet-scented apple crumble.*

RECHTE SEITE: *Die Porzellanschüssel wird gleich mit duftendem, knusprigem »Apple Crumble« gefüllt.*

PAGE DE DROITE: *Tout à l'heure, le contenu de la jatte en porcelaine se transformera en un succulent «apple crumble» parfumé et croustillant.*

LEFT: *In a small ground-floor sitting room, an engraving representing the royal family – Victoria, Albert and their children – hangs above a mahogany desk of the same period.*
FACING PAGE: *In the master's bedroom of the house, a Jacobean bed with twisted uprights, a series of 17th-century engravings, and a "Psyché" mirror in the Empire style form an eclectic ensemble.*

LINKS: *In einem kleinen Salon im Erdgeschoß hängt ein Stich der Königsfamilie – Victoria, Albert und ihre Kinder – über einem Mahagoni-Sekretär aus dieser Zeit.*
RECHTE SEITE: *Im Schlafzimmer des Hausherrn lenkt das Bett im »Jacobean-Style« mit den gedrechselten Pfosten die Aufmerksamkeit auf sich. An der Wand hängt eine Serie von Stichen aus dem 17. Jahrhundert, im Hintergrund befindet sich ein »Psyché«-Spiegel im Empire-Stil.*

A GAUCHE: *Dans un petit salon du rez-de-chaussée, une gravure représentant la famille royale – Victoria, Albert et leurs enfants – est accrochée au-dessus d'un bureau en acajou de la même époque.*
PAGE DE DROITE: *Dans la chambre maîtresse, le lit jacobéen à colonnes torsadées attire toute l'attention, au détriment d'une série de gravures 17ᵉ et d'un miroir psyché de style Empire.*

LEFT: *In the octagonal pavilion – inspired by an 18th-century Dutch tea pavilion – a stuffed cow has been parked amongst 18th- and 19th-century treasures.*
FACING PAGE: *Skeel is world famous for his antiques and eccentricities. The treasures heaped in this old barouche reflect his appetite for unusual antiques.*

LINKS: *In dem achteckigen Pavillon, der sein Vorbild in den holländischen Teepavillons des 18. Jahrhunderts hat, liegt eine ausgestopfte Kuh zwischen verschiedenen Gegenständen aus dem 18. und 19. Jahrhundert – eine extravagante Idee von Keith.*
RECHTE SEITE: *Antiquitäten und Exzentrisches von Skeel haben einen internationalen Ruf. Die in einer alten Kutsche angehäuften Schätze belegen seinen Hang zu nicht alltäglichen Antiquitäten.*

A GAUCHE: *Dans le pavillon octogonal inspiré des pavillons de thé hollandais du 18ᵉ siècle, Keith, jamais à court d'idées extravagantes, a installé une vache empaillée qui semble se reposer parmi les trésors des 18ᵉ et 19ᵉ siècles.*
PAGE DE DROITE: *Skeel a acquis une renommée internationale en vendant des «antiques and eccentricities». Les trésors empilés dans une vieille calèche reflètent son goût prononcé pour les antiquités insolites.*

PEASENHALL

Keith Skeel

Suffolk

The London antique dealer Keith Skeel had often proclaimed his absolute horror of the country, until the day he visited friends in Suffolk and came upon a house that so completely enchanted him that he bought it on the spot. Peasenhall is a large white-painted building, with a magnificent wrought-iron balcony reminiscent of a Louisiana plantation house. Skeel liked everything about it – from the ample proportions of the rooms, to the French windows leading into the large garden and the overall impression of calm and luxury in a rural setting. Not content to rest on his laurels, within the first few months he had added a greenhouse in the purest Victorian style, a grotto adorned with seashells and a fountain, along with a gazebo, statues and antique garden furniture. In short, he turned the place into an earthly paradise for a Noah's Ark of inhabitants, who came to include Gertrude (a goat), Honeybuns (a rabbit) and Hansel and Gretel (a couple of pugs). Inside the house, the tone is eclectic; Keith loves to accumulate treasures, so the rooms are full of beautiful old furniture, silver, 18th- and 19th-century engravings and boxes full of rare kitchen utensils. All are assembled with the innate sense of panache and theatre that characterises Skeel's flamboyant personality.

A 19th-century earthenware blackamoor serves as a fruit stand, with a basket of bananas, apples and pears.

Ein »Mohr« aus Keramik aus dem 19. Jahrhundert bietet lächelnd appetitliches Obst an.

Un «blackamoor» en faïence du 19ᵉ fait office de jardinière et présente – avec le sourire – sa belle récolte de fruits.

Der Londoner Antiquitätenhändler Keith Skeel hatte oft
behauptet, daß das Landleben ihm ein Graus sei. Doch als er
eines Tages Freunde in Suffolk besuchte, fand er ein Anwesen,
das ihn so ansprach, daß er es auf der Stelle kaufte! Das große
weiße Haus mit der kunstvollen schmiedeeisernen Balkonbrü-
stung, die an die prächtigen Herrenhäuser in Louisiana erinnert, verfügte über alles, was Keith gefiel: Zimmer von riesigen
Ausmaßen, Balkonfenster mit Aussicht auf einen großen Garten und den Luxus der Stille rundherum. Da der ausgespro-
chen kreative Skeel sich nicht gerne auf seinen Lorbeeren aus-
ruht, baute er bereits in den ersten Monaten ein Treibhaus im
viktorianischen Stil und eine mit Muscheln sowie einem
Springbrunnen verzierte Grotte an. Im Garten errichtete er
einen Pavillon und stellte Statuen sowie antike Gartenmöbel
auf – kurz: Es entstand ein Paradies auf Erden für die Bewohner dieser Arche Noah, wie etwa die Ziege Gertrud, den Hasen
Honeybuns und das Mopspärchen Hänsel und Gretel. Da
Keith es liebt, »Schätze« anzuhäufen, finden sich schöne antike
Möbel, Silberbesteck, Gemälde und Stiche aus dem 18. und
19. Jahrhundert sowie ein Sammelsurium von seltenen
Küchengeräten. »Zusammenführung« nennt das Skeel, mit
einem gewissen Sinn für Theatralik, die typisch ist für dynami-
sche Persönlichkeiten wie ihn.

*Gertrude the goat is
visibly puzzled by the
conduct of a gamecock.*

*Wie jede Engländerin
staunt die Ziege Ger-
trud über den kessen
französischen Hahn.*

*Gertrud la chèvre, com-
me chaque Anglais(e)
qui se respecte, s'étonne
de l'audace du coq fran-
çais.*

Jadis, l'antiquaire londonien Keith Skeel clamait son profond
dégoût pour les «charmes» de la campagne, mais un beau jour,
en rendant visite à quelques amis dans le Suffolk, il s'est trouvé
face à une demeure qui l'a tellement fasciné qu'il l'a acquise sur
le champ! La grande maison blanche, ornée d'un magnifique
balcon en ferronnerie, réminiscence des demeures somptueuses
de Louisiane, avait tout pour plaire à Keith – surtout les pièces
aux dimensions impressionnantes et les portes-fenêtres don-
nant sur un vaste jardin, et puis elle offrait le luxe de vivre au
calme – mais comme ce créateur invétéré n'aime pas se reposer
sur ses lauriers, il y a ajouté, dès les premiers mois, une serre
dans le plus pur style victorien, une grotte ornée de coquilles et
une fontaine, et a peuplé le jardin d'un «gazebo», de statues et
de meubles de jardin anciens. Bref, un petit paradis terrestre
qui sert de territoire à une véritable arche de Noé où l'on
remarque surtout Gertrud la chèvre, Honeybuns le lapin et les
carlins Hansl et Gretl. A l'intérieur, le ton est à l'éclectisme et
comme Keith adore l'amoncellement de «trésors», on y trouve
de très beaux meubles anciens, de l'argenterie, des tableaux et
des gravures du 18ᵉ et du 19ᵉ siècles et de rares ustensiles de
cuisine en vrac! Rassemblés, cela va de soi, en montrant un
penchant pour l'effet théâtral et avec le panache qui caractérise
sa personnalité flamboyante.

*Peasenhall is a proud
Victorian estate in the
heart of Suffolk.*

*Peasenhall ist ein stolzer
viktorianischer Bau im
Herzen von Suffolk.*

*Peasenhall est une fière
demeure victorienne,
plantée au cœur du
Suffolk.*

LEFT: *The rattan arm-chair is in perfect harmony with the décor of grotesques in the greenhouse.*

FACING PAGE: *Beneath the wrought-iron arbour, lit by a small crystal chandelier, a green and white rattan table and chairs await the guests who will sit down to this light collation.*

LINKS: *Der viktorianische Korbsessel harmoniert perfekt mit den »bizarren« Elementen des Gewächshauses.*

RECHTE SEITE: *Unter dem schmiedeeisernen Gewölbe der Gartenlaube, die ein kleiner Kristallüster schmückt, laden grünweiße Korbmöbel zu einen kleinen Imbiss »al fresco« ein.*

A GAUCHE: *Le fauteuil en rotin victorien s'harmonise parfaitement avec le décor à grotesques de la serre.*

PAGE DE DROITE: *Sous la tonnelle en fer forgé agrémentée d'un petit lustre en cristal, une table et des chaises en rotin vert et blanc attendent les invités qui s'attableront devant cette petite collation «al fresco».*

"Stands the church clock still at ten to three?
And is there honey still for tea?"

»Steht die Uhr auf zehn vor vier?
Und haben wir zum Tee noch Honig hier?«

«Est-il bien trois heures moins dix au clocher?
Et y a-t-il encore du miel pour le thé?»

RUPERT BROOKE
The Old Vicarage, Grantchester

ABOVE: *still life by an anonymous artist with a depiction of The Supper at Emmaus in the background (c. 1600–1610), private collection.*

OBEN: *Stilleben eines anonymen Meisters mit einer Darstellung von Christus in Emmaus im Hintergrund (um 1600–1610), Privatbesitz.*

CI-DESSUS: *nature morte d'un peintre anonyme avec la Cène à Emmaüs en arrière-plan (vers 1600–1610), collection particulière.*

FACING PAGE: *"The Animals' Banquet", a charming tableau set in a pavilion at Peasenhall, which brings together antiques, eccentricities and stuffed animals. Even the drowsy Dalmatian dates from the 19th century.*

RECHTE SEITE: *»Das Bankett der Tiere« ist eine charmante Komposition aus Antiquitäten, Raritäten und ausgestopften Tieren in einem der Pavillons von Peasenhall. Sogar der dösende Dalmatiner stammt aus dem 19. Jahrhundert!*

PAGE DE DROITE: *«Le Banquet des animaux», petit tableau charmant mis en scène dans un pavillon de Peasenhall et qui réunit antiquités, excentricités et animaux empaillés. Même le dalmatien qui somnole date du 19e!*

PREVIOUS PAGES: *On an old bench in the garden, Hansel studiously ignores the rooster.* LEFT: *Keith never tires of his bizarre tableaux. Here a stuffed monkey fills the role of a 17th-century portraitist.* FACING PAGE: *The library on the ground floor has all the props of the old-fashioned gentleman-scholar: telescope, globe, mirror ball and antiquarian books.*

VORHERGEHENDE DOPPELSEITE: *Hänsel ignoriert den stolzen Hahn, mit dem er die Gartenbank teilen muß…* LINKS: *Keith ergreift jede Gelegenheit zu bizarren Szenerien: Hier spielt der ausgestopfte Affe einen Porträtmaler aus dem 17. Jahrhundert.* RECHTE SEITE: *Die Bibliothek im Erdgeschoß gleicht dem Refugium eines Gelehrten: ein Fernrohr, ein Globus, eine Glaskugel mit Quecksilberverspiegelung und antike Bücher.*

DOUBLE PAGE PRÉCÉDENTE: *Sur un vieux banc de jardin, Hansl préfère ignorer le coq à l'allure fière avec lequel il doit partager sa couche…* A GAUCHE: *Keith ne se lasse jamais des scènes bizarres. Ici, le singe empaillé joue les portraitistes du 17e siècle.* PAGE DE DROITE: *La bibliothèque du rez-de-chaussée a vraiment tout de l'antre du savant: une longue-vue, un globe terrestre, une boule argentée au mercure et des livres anciens.*

LEFT: *At Peasenhall, Keith has again demonstrated his flair for authentic-looking kitchens. The cupboards, which come from an old shop, are filled with 19th-century porcelain and earthenware. An old draper's table and a butcher's block provide working surfaces.*
FACING PAGE: *Time for drinks: Hansel guards the decanter of white wine.*

LINKS: *In Peasenhall konnte Keith wieder einmal sein Talent für eine authentisch wirkende Küchengestaltung unter Beweis stellen: Schränke aus einem alten Geschäft sind reich mit Porzellan und Keramik aus dem 19. Jahrhundert gefüllt; ein alter Tisch aus einer Tuchhandlung und ein »Butcher's Block« werden als Arbeitsfläche genutzt.*
RECHTE SEITE: *Es ist Zeit für den Apéritif… Hänsel ist auf den Tisch geklettert, um seinen Anteil einzufordern.*

A GAUCHE: *A Peasenhall, Keith a su prouver, une fois de plus, son talent pour installer des cuisines qui étonnent par leur aspect authentique. Des armoires provenant d'un ancien magasin regorgent de porcelaines et de faïences 19ᵉ, une ancienne table de drapier et un «butcher's block» forment le plan de travail.*
PAGE DE DROITE: *C'est l'heure de l'apéritif et Hansl est monté sur la table pour participer à la cérémonie.*

ABOVE: *In the bedroom, the bedhead is a piece of Louis Quinze woodwork. Keith loves baroque things and this taste is reflected in his choice of pedestal table, the bench at the foot of the bed and the white and gold bedside table.*

RIGHT: *In the drawing room, a pensive-looking 19th-century marble cherub loiters between a couple of Victorian bookcases.*

FACING PAGE: *In the bathroom, Keith has opted for sober black and white. The tiled floor is original, as are the washbasin and taps.*

OBEN: *Das Kopfteil des Bettes besteht aus einem Holzpaneel im Louis-Quinze-Stil. Keith liebt Barockes, was das runde Tischchen, die Bank und der Nachttisch beweisen.*

RECHTS: *In einem Salon steht ein Cherubim aus dem 19. Jahrhundert zwischen zwei viktorianischen Bücherschränken.*

RECHTE SEITE: *Das Bad hat Keith puristisch gestaltet: in Schwarz und Weiß. Sowohl die Steinfliesen auf dem Boden als auch das Waschbecken und die Armatur sind antik.*

CI-DESSUS: *La tête du lit est un élément de boiserie de style Louis Quinze. Keith adore les formes baroques et son goût se reflète dans le choix du guéridon, de la banquette et de la table de nuit.*

A DROITE: *Dans le salon, un chérubin en marbre 19ᵉ exprime sa mélancolie entre deux armoires victoriennes.*

PAGE DE DROITE: *Pour sa salle de bains, Keith a choisi une palette sobre toute de blanc et de noir. Le sol à cabochons est ancien ainsi que le lavabo et la robinetterie.*

GRIMSTON PARK

Yorkshire

The people who live in the west wing of Grimston Park were only too aware that the acquisition of even a modest slice of this palatial, Italianate country house was something of a leap in the dark. Grimston is a remarkable building surrounded by rolling parkland, majestic trees, statuary and assorted follies; the second Lord Howden had it built by the celebrated architect Decimus Burton between 1840 and 1850, in a vain attempt to salvage his marriage to the fabulously wealthy Princess Bagration – "La Belle Bagration" – and spent a fortune in the process. Today, the ruined remains of the greenhouse are there to remind us that despite Grimston's romantic aspect, its days of glory are long gone. Nevertheless, the family that uses the Yellow Drawing Room with its lofty columns and ceiling covered in arabesques, and whose tea is taken in the Blue Room with its pale azure Chinese wallpaper, has managed to create an atmosphere of the utmost cosiness. The sofas are comfortable, the furniture is classical, as it should be, and above all there is no trace of ostentation or pretentiousness. The great rooms no longer stand empty and silent; instead they echo with the sounds of children, dogs and crackling wood fires.

ABOVE: *the owner, in the stables with one of her favourite horses.*
LEFT: *the trunk of a very old tree in the park at Grimston.*

OBEN: *die Hausherrin mit ihrem Lieblings-pferd vor dem Stall.*
LINKS: *Im Park gibt es einen majestätischen alten Baum mit ein-drucksvollem Stamm und Wurzeln zu ent-decken.*

CI-DESSUS: *la maî-tresse de maison devant les écuries avec son che-val favori.*
A GAUCHE: *Dans le parc, un vieil arbre majestueux expose son tronc aux racines impressionnantes.*

Die Bewohner des Westflügels des Herrenhauses waren sich durchaus im klaren darüber, daß der Kauf auch nur eines kleinen Teils des palastartigen Baus viel Mut erfordert. Dieses imposante Gebäude wurde zwischen 1840 und 1850 nach italienischem Vorbild für den zweiten Lord Howden von dem berühmten Architekten Decimus Burton umgebaut. Grimston Park ist ein Traum, umgeben von einem riesigem Park mit vielen Statuen und Pavillons. Lord Howden steckte ein Vermögen in den Bau in dem verzweifelten Versuch, seine Ehe mit der reichen Prinzessin Bagration zu retten, die auch die »schöne Bagration« genannt wurde. Doch heute erinnern die Überreste des Treibhauses daran, daß trotz des romantischen Flairs die Glanzzeiten des Hauses längst vorbei sind... Die Familie, die heute den wunderschönen »Yellow Drawing Room« mit den hohen Säulen und den mit Arabesken verzierten Wänden und Decken bewohnt und ihren Tee im »Blue Room« – die blaßblaue chinesische Tapete gab ihm den Namen – einnimmt, hat mit bequemen Sofas und einigen Möbeln im klassischen Stil eine behagliche Atmosphäre geschaffen. Hier ist nichts protzig oder prätentiös. Man versammelt sich um den Kamin, in dem ein Holzfeuer prasselt, und lauscht dem Lachen der Kinder und dem Hundegebell, das in den großen Salons widerhallt...

A romantic pavilion, complete with walls and pilasters crowned by classical urns, used today as a woodstore.

Eine Mauer mit urnenbekrönten Pilastern säumt den romantischen Pavillon, der heute als Schuppen für das Kaminholz dient.

Aujourd'hui, un pavillon romantique encerclé de murs et de pilastres couronnés d'urnes classiques sert de remise pour le bois de chauffage...

Les habitants de l'aile ouest du manoir de Grimston Park réalisent bien que l'acquisition d'un partie – modeste – de cette propriété palatiale a été un véritable acte de courage, car mettre le doigt dans cette imposante demeure italianisante, transformée entre 1840 et 1850 par le célèbre architecte Decimus Burton pour le second Lord Howden, touchait à la folie. Grimston Park est une merveille. Entourée d'un parc planté d'arbres aux dimensions impressionnantes et parsemée de statues et de petits pavillons, la demeure est le témoin muet d'un époque où Lord Howden, essayant de sauver son mariage avec la richissime princesse Bagration – la Belle Bagration – dépensa une fortune pour la construire. Aujourd'hui la serre en ruine nous rappelle que malgré son aspect romantique, les jours de gloire de la maison sont bien loin... La famille, qui occupe aujourd'hui le magnifique «Yellow Drawing Room» avec ses hautes colonnes et son plafond et ses murs décorés d'arabesques et qui prend le thé dans le «Blue Room» – tendu d'un papier peint chinois bleu pâle qui lui a donné son nom –, a créé une ambiance très cosy en introduisant des canapés confortables et quelques meubles aux lignes classiques. Rien d'ostentatoire ni de prétentieux. On se réunit autour d'un feu de bois qui crépite et les grands salons résonnent des éclats de rire des enfants et des aboiements des chiens...

The west wing of Grimston Park is extended by a large orangery.

Der Westflügel von Grimston Park erstreckt sich bis zu einer weitläufigen Orangerie.

L'aile ouest de Grimston Park est prolongé par les vestiges d'une orangerie aux proportions généreuses.

LEFT: *In the main drawing room, the classical furniture is in perfect harmony with the lavish red and gold décor.*
FACING PAGE: *The wall decorations are of exquisite quality, with mythical creatures and garlands of flowers framing the wooden panelling.*

LINKS: *Im großen Salon harmonieren die klassizistischen Möbel mit dem üppigen Dekor in Rot und Gold.*
RECHTE SEITE: *Die Wanddekoration ist von unvergleichlicher Schönheit. Phantastische Tiere und Blumengirlanden zieren die Bordüren der Vertäfelungen.*

A GAUCHE: *Dans le grand salon, le mobilier classique s'harmonise à la perfection avec le décor somptueux rouge et or.*
PAGE DE DROITE: *Les décorations murales sont d'une qualité incomparable. Des animaux fantastiques et des guirlandes de fleurs ornent les bordures des lambris.*

ACKNOWLEDGEMENTS
DANKSAGUNG
REMERCIEMENTS

It is difficult not simply to repeat the acknowledgements made in "Country Houses of France". Ursula Fethke has assembled the text with her customary sensitivity and precision, and we are most grateful to her – and to her team of translators – for extracting the very best from the material we provided. Last but not least, we would like to thank all those who opened their doors to us and made this book possible. Finally, we are most grateful for the invaluable advice and support of Min Hogg (The World of Interiors) and Elfreda Pownall (Sunday Telegraph Magazine).

Es ist gar nicht leicht, nicht einfach die Danksagung für »Landhäuser in Frankreich« zu wiederholen. Ursula Fethke hat sich mit gewohnter Sympathie und Präzision in die Texte vertieft und so – unterstützt von einem talentierten Team und intelligenten sensiblen Übersetzern – den besten Teil des Materials, das sich auf ihrem Schreibtisch stapelte, herausgefiltert. Es bleibt uns – last but not least – ein großes Dankeschön all denjenigen auszusprechen, die uns ihre Türen geöffnet haben. Ein besonderer Dank gilt auch Min Hogg von »The World of Interiors« und Elfreda Pownall vom »Sunday Telegraph Magazine«, die uns in ihrem Adreßbuch blättern ließen.

Il est difficile de ne pas se répéter après les remerciements parus dans «Les Maisons romantiques de France». Comme d'habitude, Ursula Fethke s'est penchée sur le texte avec la même sympathie et la même précision et – aidée par une équipe de talent et par des traducteurs intelligents et sensibles – elle a su tirer le meilleur parti du matériel qui s'empilait sur son bureau. Il nous reste, last but not least, à dire un grand merci à tous ceux qui nous ouvrirent leur porte. Nous tenons également à exprimer notre reconnaissance à Min Hogg de «The World of Interiors» et Elfreda Pownall du «Sunday Telegraph Magazine» qui nous ont laissé puiser librement dans leur carnet d'adresses.

Barbara & René Stoeltie

FRONT COVER: *In a pavilion at Peasenhall, Suffolk (see pages 172–185)*

UMSCHLAGVORDERSEITE: *In einem Pavillon von Peasenhall, Suffolk (siehe Seite 172–185)*

COUVERTURE: *Dans un pavillon de Peasenhall, Suffolk (voir pages 172–185)*

BACK COVER: *Detail of Loudham Hall, Suffolk (see pages 160–171)*

UMSCHLAGRÜCKSEITE: *Detailansicht aus Loudham Hall, Suffolk (siehe Seite 160–171)*

DOS DE COUVERTURE: *Détail de Loudham Hall, Suffolk (voir pages 160–171)*

ENDPAPERS: *Detail of the colonnade at West Wycombe Park, Buckinghamshire (see pages 124–137)*

VORSATZPAPIER: *Detail des Säulengangs von West Wycombe Park, Buckinghamshire (siehe Seite 124–137)*

PAGES DE GARDE: *Détail de la colonnade de West Wycombe Park, Buckinghamshire (voir pages 124–137)*

PAGE 2: *Teatime at Peasenhall, Suffolk*

SEITE 2: *Teatime in Peasenhall, Suffolk*

PAGE 2: *A l'heure du thé, Peasenhall, Suffolk*

PAGE 4: *Thomas Gainsborough, Margaret and Mary Gainsborough (c. 1770), Whitbread Collection, Southhill*

SEITE 4: *Thomas Gainsborough, Margaret und Mary Gainsborough (ca. 1770), Whitbread Collection, Southhill*

PAGE 4: *Thomas Gainsborough, Margaret et Mary Gainsborough (vers 1770), Whitbread Collection, Southhill*

PAGE 15: *The portrait of Jane Austen was taken from the book:*

SEITE 15: *Das Porträt von Jane Austen stammt aus dem Buch:*

PAGE 15: *Le portrait de Jane Austen est extrait du livre:*

James Edward Austen-Leigh, A Memoir of Jane Austen, London 1870

PAGE 190: *Jean-Michel Picart, Bunch of flowers on a balustrade (1653), Karlsruhe, Staatliche Kunsthalle*

SEITE 190: *Jean-Michel Picart, Blumenstrauß auf einer Brüstung (1653), Karlsruhe, Staatliche Kunsthalle*

PAGE 190: *Jean-Michel Picart, Bouquet sur une balustrade (1653), Karlsruhe, Staatliche Kunsthalle*

© 1999 Benedikt Taschen Verlag GmbH
Hohenzollernring 53, D–50672 Köln
© 1999 VG Bild-Kunst, Bonn, for the work by Pierre Alechinsky
Design by Catinka Keul, Cologne
Layout by Angelika Taschen, Cologne
Texts edited by Ursula Fethke, Cologne, Elke Eßmann, Dortmund
Lithography by Ute Wachendorf, Cologne
English translation by Anthony Roberts, Lupiac
German translation by Marion Valentin, Cologne

ISBN 3-8228-6526-5 (edition with English cover)
ISBN 3-8228-6575-3 (edition with German cover)
ISBN 3-8228-0793-1 (edition with French cover)